"We all live impossible lives. What Bob Beaudine does in *2 Chairs* is show us that we don't have to do it ourselves. God is ready, able, and willing to meet us every morning and swap our cares for His power!"

—Scott Drew, Head Men's Basketball Coach, Baylor University

"Bob Beaudine fires me up! The sheer force of his personality influences so many, and the secret of his life is found in *2 Chairs*. If you want to live with peace, purpose, and happiness and to make a positive difference in others for good, read this book. I can't think of anything more important than learning and living the message of this book."

—**Jack Graham**, Pastor, Prestonwood Baptist Church

"Bob Beaudine teaches us to never look at a chair the same way again. Sit down and be prepared for Who will show up. It just may change your life!"

—**David Pack**, GRAMMY Award–Winning Recording Artist,
Producer, Saddleback Church/Rick Warren Ministries,
Artist for PEACE

"I hope and pray that the 'secret' Bob shares in this book would become not-so-secret. It has the potential to change your life!"

—**Mark Batterson**, *New York Times* Best-Selling Author of
The Circle Maker, Lead Pastor of National Community Church

"The most influential man in sports you've never heard of."

—*Sports Illustrated*

"Once again Bob Beaudine has stopped me in my tracks with his profound yet simple grasp of what is most important. In the spirit of J. B. Phillips's *Your God Is Too Small*, Bob reminds us that our thinking and faith are too small, not God. Read this book and be refreshed, then read it again."

—**Eric Affeldt**, former President and CEO, ClubCorp

"*2 Chairs* is the answer to the pace of the world, the noise that surrounds our lives, and the difficulty in finding peace."

—**Scott O'Neil**, CEO, Philadelphia 76ers and New Jersey Devils

"I smiled and teared all the way to the 'called shot' in the corner pocket! Thanks for helping me arrange the meeting of a lifetime. I feel like the comfort and clarity for the frustrations of life are just a morning away."

—**Ryan Binkley**, CEO, Generational Equity,
and Lead Pastor, Create Church

"Success follows a great game plan. My friend Bob Beaudine gives us a great one in *2 Chairs*—teaching us to win each day by starting with God."

—**Tubby Smith**, NCAA Champion Basketball Coach

"Have you been seeking the one thing that will make a difference in your life? Then dig in to Bob Beaudine's latest book, *2 Chairs*, to implement the secret that changes everything. You'll be eternally grateful."

—**Susan B. Mead**, A Top 100 Christian Blogger,
Best-Selling Author of *Dance with Jesus: From Grief to Grace*

"I have been in business for almost three decades and in that time no one has been more impactful to my team and to me personally. I think about Bob's amazing lessons from the time I wake up to the time I go to sleep. This man and this book is a GAME CHANGER!"

—**Larry North**, Nationally Renowned Fitness Executive,

Speaker, Author, and Radio Host

"Bob Beaudine is a tremendous learner, and as a result is also a tremendous teacher. He's able to take complex topics and break them into simple and actionable life-changing lessons. *2 Chairs* is another great demonstration of Bob's ability to inspire thought and teach valuable insights."

—**Tom Garfinkel**, President and CEO, Miami Dolphins

"Bob Beaudine just took *The Power of WHO!* to a whole different level. This book is going to help multitudes of people finally understand how to get connected to the most important 'Who' of their lives and why it is so important to establish this connection. What a brilliant and life-giving message for the masses!"

—**Danny McDaniel**, Triple Diamond and

Hall of Fame Distributor, AdvoCare, Intl.

"The greatest ideas are the simplest. This book offers a great yet simple invitation. I hope you will accept it. *2 Chairs* moments can change a life."

—**Max Lucado**, Pastor and Best-Selling Author of *Glory Days*

"*2 Chairs* is a definitive road map to personal transformation. Bob Beaudine's profound insights are anchored by the transcendent realities of the human soul. In *2 Chairs* he not only guides every reader toward a fresh and fantastic future, but more importantly offers spiritual keys to unlock the inner strength needed for following this remarkable road. *2 Chairs* is indispensable to all who seek their true destiny."

—**Rabbi Daniel Lapin**, President, the American Alliance of Jews and Christians, Author of *Business Secrets from the Bible*

"A month ago I was overwhelmed with life's circumstances. *2 Chairs* and 30 days later I am overwhelmed with His blessing."

—**Tom Ziglar**, Proud Son of Zig Ziglar and CEO, Zig Ziglar Corporation

"The world is a dangerous place; we all need *2 Chairs*."

—**LCDR Mark McGinnis**, Managing Director, SEAL Legacy Foundation, Former US Navy SEAL Commander

"We restore houses; God restores lives. Discover the blueprint for God's restoration in the pages of *2 Chairs*."

—**Chip and Joanna Gaines**, Magnolia Homes, Stars of HGTV's *Fixer Upper*

"I love Bob, this book, and his 'three simple but disruptive questions' to help make an everlasting impact on your life."

—**Marc Kidd**, CEO, Captivate Network

"In a word—Wow! *2 Chairs* is a game changer and a life-changing experience! I couldn't put the book down. God has gifted Bob with the ability to teach and inspire."

—**Tony Orlando**, GRAMMY Award Winner,

Legendary Music Artist

"Yesterday my son finished the *2 Chairs* experience to discover God's good plan for a job. He not only found a great job but knows this is the place God wants and has prepared him to be. All you and I need is one more chair, and the same can be true for us."

—**Randy Frazee**, former Senior Pastor, Oak Hills Church;

former Teaching Pastor, Willow Creek Community Church

Author of *Believe* and *The Heart of the Story*

"As an athlete, I can tell you that preparation is the key to success, and there is no better preparation for the day than starting with God."

—**Shane Doan**, Captain of the Arizona Coyotes,

Longest-Serving Captain in the NHL

"As an executive, author, and speaker, Bob Beaudine has focused on one of life's deepest issues—relationships. His first book, *The Power of WHO!*, was about the importance of friends. In *2 Chairs*, he raises the stakes and writes about our relationship with God—nothing could be of greater value."

—**Jerry Colangelo**, Chairman, USA Basketball,

Former Owner, Phoenix Suns and Arizona Diamondbacks

"In *2 Chairs*, Bob Beaudine helps us all to unlock the essence of our spiritual lives and our relationship with our Creator. His advice is simple and powerful. Bob's life work has been to improve the lives of others—he has done it for me and my loved ones, and now in this book he will do it for you!"

—**Chester Elton**, Best-Selling Author of *The Carrot Principle*, *All In*, and *What Motivates Me*

"Seeking to hear from God every morning at *2 Chairs* is a message everyone needs to hear."

—**Steve Douglass**, President, Campus Crusade for Christ International/Cru

"Starting every morning at 2 Chairs is a critical piece in fulfilling our God-given promise."

—**Bill McCartney**, National Champion NCAA Football coach, University of Colorado, and Founder of Promise Keepers

"Years ago, I got in the habit of starting my day with a cup of coffee on my back deck, watching the sun come up and spending the first part of my day with God. I don't get out there every day, but the days I do just seem to go smoother. It's as though that one-on-one time with God sets the tone for my whole day. That's the spirit behind Bob Beaudine's *2 Chairs*. It's a simple way to connect with God—and to let Him connect with you."

—**Dave Ramsey**, Number-One Best-Selling Author, Nationally Syndicated Radio Show Host

"Regardless of your age, gender, career path, or where you are on the economic ladder, you will find *2 Chairs* to be an important and timely message. With everything going on in our world, there is no time like the present to set up your *2 Chairs* and begin each day in the presence of God."

—**Josh McDowell**, Best-Selling Author, Speaker, President of Josh McDowell Ministries

"I was privileged to know Bob Beaudine's mom, Martha. She shared a 'secret' with Bob about God that he has been practicing for forty years. Bob now shares that secret with us in his new book, *2 Chairs*. Thank you, Martha, for this wonderful gift!"

—**Bob Tiede**, Author, *Great Leaders Ask Questions*, U.S. Leadership Development Team, Campus Crusade

"I love this book. It will impact a lot of hurting people who don't know where to turn."

—**Ray Davis**, Owner of the Texas Rangers

"FANTASTIC, LIFE CHANGING, LIFE SAVING."

—**John Cahill**, President, La Madeleine Restaurants

"I am a huge Bob Beaudine fan! In *2 Chairs*, Bob challenges us to have an amazing journey with God through his practical and passionate insights. A must read."

—**Todd Graham**, Head Football Coach, Arizona State University

2
CHAIRS

2 CHAIRS

THE SECRET THAT CHANGES EVERYTHING

BOB BEAUDINE

WORTHY®
PUBLISHING

Worthy
Hachette Book Group
1290 Avenue of the Americas, New York, NY 10104
worthypublishing.com
twitter.com/worthypub

First trade paperback edition: January 2018 | First hardcover edition: August 2016

Worthy is a division of Hachette Book Group, Inc. The Worthy name and logo are trademarks of Hachette Book Group, Inc.

The publisher is not responsible for websites (or their content) that are not owned by the publisher. | Unless otherwise noted, Scripture quotations are taken from the Holy Bible, *New International Version®, NIV®*. Copyright © 1973, 1978, 1984 by Biblica, Inc.™ Used by permission of Zondervan. All rights reserved worldwide. | Scripture quotations marked KJV are taken from the King James Version of the Bible. Public domain. | Scripture quotations marked NIV are taken from THE HOLY BIBLE, NEW INTERNATIONAL VERSION®, NIV® Copyright © 1973, 1978, 1984, 2011 by Biblica, Inc.® Used by permission. All rights reserved worldwide.

Library of Congress Cataloging-in-Publication Data
Names: Beaudine, Bob, author.
Title: 2 chairs : the secret that changes everything / Bob Beaudine.
Other titles: Two chairs
Description: Franklin, TN : Worthy Publishing, 2016.
Identifiers: LCCN 2016018066 | ISBN 9781617958014 (hardcover)
Subjects: LCSH: Problem solving—Religious aspects—Christianity. |
    Spirituality—Christianity. | Spiritual life—Christianity. | Providence
    and government of God—Christianity.
Classification: LCC BV4599.5.P75 B43 2016 | DDC 248.8/6--dc23
LC record available at https://lccn.loc.gov/2016018066

Print book interior design by Bart Dawson.

ISBN: 978-1-68397-253-2 (trade paperback), 978-1-61795-801-4 (hardcover),
978-1-61795-869-4 (e-book)

Printed in the United States of America
LSC-C
10 9 8 7 6 5

To all the moms who have guided the spiritual health
of their families when no one else stepped up.
And most especially to mine,
Martha Beaudine—I love you and miss you every day.

CONTENTS

INTRODUCTION

Since 1976, I have been having the same meeting each and every morning for mentoring, advice, and daily guidance. It's been life changing! Looking back, I can clearly see that all my success in business and life, as well as getting through the hardest of times, points back to these special meetings. Sometimes they lasted only five minutes while others flashed by in an hour. People talk about having life coaches or being part of a mastermind networking group, but this is so much more. Here each morning a strategic transfer takes place. And the resulting peace, joy, insight, wisdom, power, and favor shared with me each day has changed the entire trajectory of my life and continues to do so today. I have to tell you, I could never imagine missing this morning chat.

My dad helped start the executive search industry back in the 1960s out of McKinsey & Co. He was a brilliant man, my best friend, and professional mentor. In my career, I've had the opportunity to sit and interview presidents of the United States, generals, titans of industry, and Hall of Fame coaches. But the greatest advice in life or business ever passed on to me was actually given to me by my mom, the late Martha Beaudine, back in 1976. She told me of a "secret" that was passed on to her, a secret I didn't even know was a possibility. One you might not know of either. As she talked about it, there was a serious tone in her voice, a passion, a glow that radiated from her. She seemed so honored to share this precious gift with me. She declared, "There is nothing that you could do or think of in life, Bob, that would be more important than setting up your two chairs right now and doing it every day of your life."

What's the *secret*? Well, what she shared with me that day is not only a secret but also a supernatural truth. Now you might be thinking, *Why was his mom talking about chairs being the secret to the universe?* Well, it's not about furniture; it's about Who will be sitting with you in the furniture.

The secret that Mom was talking about is this: God wants to spend time with each of us every morning, before we begin the day. He wants to talk to us, to be friends. He already knows everything about us, and He wants us to know everything about Him.

When my mom first introduced me to *"2 Chairs,"* it was a great time for me to hear about this opportunity because, as a soon-to-be college graduate, I had a bunch of questions about life goals, dreams, obstacles, finding a mate, and getting a job. And I needed answers. Even though my dad was my normal go-to guy for subjects like this, my mom always offered me a unique, spiritual insight that I hadn't heard from others, and what she said intrigued me.

When I was growing up, Mom would always remind me that I had an assignment, a purpose, and a destiny all my own that I needed to discover. But this encouraging thought also perplexed me because I didn't know what my calling in life could possibly be or how I would ever discover it. My mom didn't have all the answers, but she knew where I could find them.

> **I didn't know what my calling in life could possibly be or how I would ever discover it. My mom didn't have all the answers, but she knew where I could find them.**

Over the years, I have wondered if anyone else has discovered what my mom introduced to me. I found out by studying history, reading biographies, and talking with others that the answer is *yes!* The stories I read and heard didn't use the term *2 Chairs*, but the description of the moments these people experienced on a regular basis, as well as with whom they met, was always starkly similar. The puzzling question for me is, *Why don't more people talk about this?*

I'm sure as you're reading this, you have the same questions I had when I first heard about *2 Chairs*—questions like:

- Why two chairs—who sits in the other one?
- What's the point of the meeting?
- What will be discussed?
- How often do I need to meet?
- I have enough meetings already—how can I fit in any more?
- How long will this take?

These are all natural questions, but the answers are much deeper than you think. If you're like most people, you're probably thinking, *Who has the time or energy for deep thinking, deep reflection, or deep anything?* But don't allow yourself to go there, because deep down you know something is wrong. It might be something small or something big, but you know you don't have an answer for it. You've come to a realization there is a limit to what you can do on your own.

My mom came to understand her own limitations and

turned it into a strategic advantage the rest of her life. She would always tell me that in this life you will have trouble. It's unfortunately one of the common bonds we all share. Life will be crazy, painful, messy, and suddenly tragic. Often you don't cause it, sometimes you do. Regardless of how it arrives, you must be prepared. This is where asking good questions becomes a difference maker.

Have you noticed, however, that when things are going your way, you don't spend a lot of time asking a lot of questions? In fact, you want to "knock on wood," not rock the boat, and hope life can just stay good. But we all know this kind of naïve thinking leads to problems.

On one hand, you face some problems that you confidently believe you can and should handle yourself: a broken garage door, a flooded bathroom, a kid sick again at daycare, or that one person at

You've come to a realization there is a limit to what you can do on your own.

work who doesn't seem to like you no matter what you do or say. But on the other hand, there are other problems that bring so much trouble to your heart that you don't know what to do or where to turn: an accident, a job loss, a bad health prognosis, divorce papers served, or a son or daughter in trouble. In times like these, it is easy to isolate yourself and start feeling hopeless. If you're truly honest with yourself, you'll admit that you have a lot more of the second kind of problems than you'd ever want to tell anyone about. That's why you need something bigger than who you are—bigger than your thoughts, your ways, and clearly bigger than any trouble that hits you square between the eyes.

Believe me when I tell you, *2 Chairs* is what you've needed all along!

I'll never forget my first *2 Chairs* moment; it changed my life forever. I already had a perfect spot in my apartment that was quiet—and there were already two chairs there that my mom had bought me several years back. Hmm ... now that I think about it, I wonder if she bought those chairs for me intentionally and had been praying that I would go there for this specific purpose one day? Knowing my mom, the answer is yes! Moms are sneaky in this way, aren't they?

I didn't really know what the first meeting would be like, except that Mom had said, "Go with the expectation that He's been waiting for this moment with you for a long time now."

I said, "Really?"

She nodded and said, "You'll see."

I had just one more question for my mom: "How should I start out a conversation with God?"

"Just be you, Bob," she said. "Say good morning, thank

Him for coming, and tell Him you have some questions. He'll take over from there."

The next morning, I woke up at 5:00 a.m. with great anticipation. Before I sat down I made myself a cup of coffee, as my mom had told me this would be like meeting with a close friend. The moment I sat down at *2 Chairs*, I felt Him. I can only describe it as a wave of peace and love that suddenly hugged me in a way, and my eyes immediately teared up. I hadn't even said anything yet. Then I clearly heard Him say in my mind, "I'm so excited you're here!"

I thought to myself, *Am I saying that?* But I knew it was Him. Our time together lasted only ten minutes, but it felt much longer. What did I feel? Well, I felt affirmed, accepted, and loved. All the big concerns that I had in my life just didn't seem so big when chatting with the God of the universe. Each time I shared with Him a concern or hurt in my life, I kept hearing Him say to me, "Give that to Me . . . yes, that too."

I finally blurted out, "What can I do for You?"

I could feel Him smile and say, "Today, just go be of good cheer. And tomorrow . . ." He paused and said, ". . . ask Me that again. You'll hear Me and know."

Maybe you're looking for answers today as I was. Whether those answers are for yourself, or for a family member or friend, chances are that's why you are holding this book. Whatever the case may be, thank you for taking the time to keep reading. Thank you for giving me the opportunity to speak into your life. Thank you for opening your mind and heart to a message that could begin to change everything for the better.

> She once asked me, "Bob, if there was a one percent chance that God would meet you, would you set up the *2 Chairs*?"

We are about to talk about some weighty topics. We are going to talk about God, family, friends, honesty, forgiveness, your mind, your heart, and any and everything in between. There will be a battle ahead for you to get through this book at times. But don't shy away. It's going to be okay. Breathe. My mom somehow knew if she could just get me to try *2 Chairs*, the enormity of what would occur would be life changing.

She once asked me, "Bob, if there was a one percent chance that God would meet you, would you set up the *2 Chairs*?"

As she said this I thought to myself, *What would I possibly have to lose by trying?* So I told her I would. My mom said that was a good decision because she believed there was a 100 percent chance He would meet me and have some things to tell me.

Over the past forty years, I've read countless books,

heard a great number of talks, and had thousands of conversations related to personal growth and spiritual matters, but I have never heard anyone approach a subject as immense and impactful as this one. I'm confident you'll come to discover what I've been reminded of every day for over forty years—my mom was right!

Once you meet with God, you'll
discover something amazing.
You'll find out He does more
than just listen to you;
He has a plan—plans
to prosper you, give you hope,
and always shed light
on your great future.
But to know these plans
you have to stop and listen.

1

THREE SIMPLE
BUT DISRUPTIVE
QUESTIONS

*God knows what you're going through, why
you're going through it and how you feel about
it. He knows you better than you know yourself.*

—RICK WARREN

I hadn't been writing this book for more than a week
when I got a call from a friend reaching out for help.
He said one of his close friends had been indicted and life
was crashing down all around him. My friend was rushing
over to meet his friend, whom he said sounded distraught,
hopeless, and possibly contemplating taking his own life. I

thought to myself, *Wow, I need to get this book done as fast as I can! This book will not only be crucial for people who are in trouble, but a great resource for all of us who just don't know what to say, what advice to give others struggling with so many issues.*

"Tell me about *2 Chairs,* Bob," he said. "What advice can I share with my friend when I get there?"

I said, "Before I explain *2 Chairs,* first make sure you give your friend a hug; he will need one. Then, tell him he's not alone. Let him know that no matter what's happened, right or wrong, you're there for him. Then go deeper. Tell him to sit down and relax for a second, because you want to help him see the field. And to get him there, you'll need to ask him three questions that will give you an opportunity to introduce him to *2 Chairs.* It's there he will find the peace, joy, insight, wisdom, power, and favor he'll need to bring back *hope* to his situation." At the end of our conversation, he felt so much better equipped to help his friend at his worst moment.

My mom approached this subject of what to do and where to turn in times of trouble by asking me three *simple yet disruptive* questions—simple in that I couldn't believe I hadn't asked them before, and disruptive because they quickly disarmed me and showcased my limitations.

The first question she asked caught me completely off guard: "Does God know your situation?"

She quickly followed up with the second question: "Is it too hard for Him to handle?" I almost asked her, "Is this too hard for *who*?" But I knew my mom was bringing a much higher perspective to my situation.

Then she asked her final question: "Does He have a good plan for you?" That question was the most disruptive, because it exposed my limitations. I believed God did have a good plan for me, but I told her I didn't know what the plan was. She replied, "Of course you don't know. That's why you need *2 Chairs!*"

QUESTION #1:
Does God know your situation?
Yes!

For some reason, when problems arise we have a tendency not to ask good questions. And even if we do, the last one it seems we want to ask is a simple one: Does God know?

I've seen it happen time after time. When people face problems beyond their ability to manage and lose control of their lives, they think that God is either too removed or too busy to even know about their situation. They act as if God is an old-time phone operator who can only handle six or seven lines for the seven billion people who are calling, and the only calls He considers important are heart attacks, terrorist strikes, and natural disasters. Others feel they have let Him down so they want to hide. Either way, they mistakenly believe they should try to handle things alone. Well, there's nothing like some trouble that forces us to our knees to ask good questions. When faced with a problem beyond our control or ability to correct ourselves, I believe this question is not only an important one, but it should be the *first* one you ask. Why? Because the answer brings everything that's out of order, back into order.

Think about the simple answer to this first question. There's something big hidden here that you need to know, and it's really comforting. What's that? *God knows!* And it's important that you know that He knows. That's why this has to be your first question. Acknowledging that God knows what's happening means believing that you are not alone. And feeling the security of the answer brings order to your situation.

The first priority for surviving a challenge, crisis, or any difficult situation is setting your mind above it, which in turn will bring clarity and perspective. What you need to do is to start at the highest thought, and of course that thought is . . . *God!* One move toward Him and He'll be all-in with you. He's not surprised or overwhelmed by your circumstance, nor is He mad or disappointed with you. He does not regret making you. Pulling up a chair and starting here changes everything.

Let me give you an example: Imagine you are the quarterback of a football team and you get sacked, rocked hard by a big defensive hit. A timeout is called and the coach and medical staff look at you on the sidelines. First, they just want to see if you're okay and will try to evaluate how badly you are hurt. They start by asking you a few simple questions to size up your condition. The answers you give will help them decide whether you're able to go back on the field or need to be held out for further examination. Now they're not going to wish or hope you're okay; they're going to be certain you're all right, because if they send you back in and you're not well, more damage can come to you and to others. Interestingly, the first question they ask isn't going to be, "Are you okay?" because people in crisis are normally in denial and will say whatever is necessary to get back in the game.

> **The first priority for surviving a challenge, crisis, or any difficult situation is setting your mind above it.**

No one goes into something expecting a negative result. When you're hit, it catches you off guard; so much so, that you will do and say the stupidest things. The coach or trainer will normally ask a few simple questions that you wouldn't expect, and he'll ask them quickly, one after another. If you're disoriented and can't answer questions like "Where are we?" "What city?" "Who are we playing?" "What's your mom's name?" everyone around you clearly sees that you aren't doing well and it's time to lock away your helmet in the equipment cart.

Asking, "Does God know your situation?" is like taking a break with the head coach to evaluate the impact of the hit you just took. It's simple and wise, yet not stopping to check your vitals first is a big mistake. Why? Because you're in a situation bigger than you can handle by yourself, and you know it. Asking this question puts everything in perspective.

It is human nature that in times of trouble (physically, professionally, or relationally) we may not want to tell family and friends about what we've done or what circumstances have hit us, so we hide and isolate ourselves out of fearfulness, humiliation, or embarrassment. But listen, that's the worst thing you can do! The good news is that God knows before you sit down. He knows your problem before you even say a word. And He's there, sitting across from you and ready to help.

If you're being rushed to the hospital by ambulance for an immediate surgery, your first thoughts won't be long-term treatment plans, physical therapy, or medicine prescriptions. No, the highest priority is to get the bleeding stopped, the heart stabilized. In other words, you're praying, "Please, God, help me survive!" So, if it's natural to start immediately with God when the issue is an emergency medical trauma, why not start with God when the crisis concerns other areas of your life such as parenting, career, finances, or emotions? It's as if we envision God having some sort of cosmic priority system in which cancer and car accidents always come before breakups and bad bosses because the former is big, important stuff worthy of God's attention and the latter is too small. Let me tell you, in the strongest possible terms, what utter nonsense this is. God knows it all, and there is nothing too small for Him. He knows the number of hairs on your head and every grain of sand on the earth—so He is fully aware and concerned about every detail of your life, big or small.

> **God knows your problem before you even say a word. And He's there, sitting across from you and ready to help.**

You can do a lot of things that seem like they would be helpful, but it is ultimately futile and even harmful to jump ahead without starting with what is foundational. First things first, and that's why this question has to be number one. It is a big thought, a foundational thought, and a reassuring thought—yes, God knows!

QUESTION #2
Is it too hard for Him to handle?
No!

For whom? God? Come on. You know better! Dr. Seuss once said, "Sometimes the questions are complicated and the answers are simple." And when it comes to life's toughest issues, you should always expect lots of complicated questions from the world around you (employers, creditors, family, friends, doctors, lawyers, and law enforcement). But don't get stuck looking for answers there, because sometimes . . . there's just no logical answer for your problem. And trying to figure it out will just wear you down and discourage you. The reason you must ask the question, "Is it too hard for Him to handle?" is to remind you what God promised in Proverbs 3:5–6: "Trust in the LORD with all your heart and lean not on your own understanding; in all your ways acknowledge him, and he will make your paths straight."

It doesn't matter if you can't see the way through your trouble, because God can! And by the way, He's not concerned, bothered, or fearful of your circumstance. Period! He's got the experience, power, and wisdom to solve it. A great word to describe Him is that He's *able*. Able to do exceedingly *and* abundantly above all that you ask or think. Able to help, keep, calm, save you in this time of trouble *and* restore you. In fact, while it is hard to believe when you are in the midst of the trouble, you will be a stronger and more compassionate person for going through this tough time of uncertainty and fear.

But before we go any further, let me remind you that even though it's not too hard for God to handle, it *is* too hard for you to handle. That's why when trouble hits, you have to run to Him as fast as you can, and only Him. Then, when you are in His presence, sitting across from Him in your *2 Chairs*, He will show you what He wants you to do. It's not too hard, but it will take faith. You have to believe! Believe that God not only *can* help you but *will* help you if you ask, seek, and knock. That's your part, believing. God calls this "faith" and says that without it, it's impossible to please Him. But for some, this concept is initially hard.

I had a friend once say to me, "I'm not sure I believe in that 'faith' stuff, Bob."

I said, "Really?" I then asked him, "Have you ever flown on a plane?"

"Sure," he said.

"Did you personally see the mechanics tighten every bolt?"

"Of course not."

I asked, "Do you really understand how a jet can one minute be in Dallas, take off, and then two hours later land in Chicago?"

He laughed and said, "I get your point. If I have the faith to get on an airplane, I have the faith to try *2 Chairs*."

I have an old college friend who grew up believing that God didn't get involved in our daily issues. He told me, "It's not that He can't or won't help, but He has too many other big issues to take care of around the world." So my friend would never ask for help.

The first time I heard him say that, I asked him, "So, if your seventeen-year-old daughter had a problem and didn't feel she should call you for help, how would you feel?"

He quickly responded, "Well she knows that I'm there for her and she'd better call."

"Really," I said. "What if she ran out of gas in the middle of nowhere? Would you want her to ask for help then?"

"Yes, of course I would."

"Now a splinter in your finger isn't a big thing, but would you help your youngest in that situation?"

"Yes!" he said.

I paused and then asked my friend, "Do you see the correlation here? God created you and spoke all throughout the Bible about wanting you to ask, seek, and knock for help whenever you're in trouble. He said that He, like a good shepherd, would leave the ninety-nine sheep to find the one that is lost. Isn't it in the small issues of life that we build trust and friendship? How could we really trust God on big things if we hadn't learned to trust Him in the small ones? Test it and see."

For many this is really hard, because the answer doesn't always come in the package or the specific timing we thought it would. As a result, we can easily be surprised, isolated, and discouraged, sometimes even feeling so hopeless that the only thing to do is quit. But you have to be careful here, because the trouble you or your loved ones are in doesn't always mean you're headed in the wrong direction. Sometimes, the trouble becomes the passageway to the answer and there's a gift waiting for you if you'll just persevere. But it will take faith to walk down this uncomfortable corridor in life, believing in something—some ONE—bigger than you. That's why it's so important for all of us to stop and talk to God first. To accept His *2 Chairs* invitation to sit and talk, spend some time together, get to know and trust Him in times like these.

So, *"Is it too hard for Him to handle?"* The simple answer is: "There's nothing too hard for God to handle," if you'll just let Him.

God created you and spoke all throughout the Bible about wanting you to ask, seek, and knock for help whenever you're in trouble.

QUESTION #3
Does He have a good plan for you?
Yes!

The answer to this is absolutely *yes!* But people in crisis respond in several ways when asked this question. Some say, "I'm not sure," which unfortunately means they don't know Him. When you don't know someone, you usually don't feel comfortable reaching out and asking for help from that person. And that's not good when you are in over your head and need a lifeline.

Others when asked, "Does God have a good plan for you?" say, "I hope so," which unfortunately sounds like they're really not sure. And whenever anyone is not sure, confusion, fear, worry, and frustration set in and surround them and their circumstances.

Finally, when someone says, "Yes, I believe that God has a good plan for me," I love to ask, "What did He say?" They say, "What do you mean, what did He say?" And this conversation then sounds a lot like the classic Abbott and Costello routine, "Who's on first?"

Have you ever seen this old comedy routine? It's genius. Bud Abbott and Lou Costello are talking about Abbott's new job as a manager of a baseball team. They're musing that baseball players have peculiar names like Dizzy Dean and his brother Daffy and their French cousin Goofé. Costello asks him if he knows the names of his infielders yet.

> Abbott: Well, let's see, we have on the bags, Who's on first, What's on second, I Don't Know is on third—
> Costello: That's what I want to find out.
> Abbott: I say Who's on first, What's on second, I Don't Know's on third.
> Costello: Are you the manager?

Abbott: Yes.

Costello: You gonna be the coach too?

Abbott: Yes.

Costello: And you don't know the fellows' names?

Abbott: Well I should.

Costello: Well then who's on first?

Abbott: Yes.

. . .

Costello: All I'm trying to find out is what's the guy's name on first base.

Abbott: No. What is on second base.

Costello: I'm not asking you who's on second.

Abbott: Who's on first.

Costello: I don't know.

Abbott: He's on third base.

I love this routine. The timing these two have and how they can make something so simple seem so confusing is genius. Unfortunately, it reminds me how confusing we have made the subject of talking and listening to God. Let me show you. When it comes to trouble in our lives, I ask these three simple but disruptive questions:

"Does God know your situation?"

"Yes."

"Is it too hard for Him to handle?"

"No."

"Does He have a good plan for you?"

"Yes."

"What is it?"

"I don't know."

"Third base!"

Third base! I think that's where many of us are today relative to our hopes, dreams, and the downright discouraging trouble we face. We are just as flat-out confused and frustrated as Lou Costello was in that comedy sketch. If we are asked any questions on our situation, our response is: "I don't know!" Exactly: "Third base!"

But let's start with what we do know. We love God, we pray, and yet many people today rush past first base each day and don't listen to *Who* is at first base—God! We think He's too busy, has bigger issues to handle, and we're not really sure He wants to meet with us. Have you ever been praying so hard to God that you didn't take the time to listen to what He had to say on the subject? Have we become so familiar with praying, doing all the talking, and not taking time to listen for God's reply? If we don't start our day at *2 Chairs,* we will find ourselves at second base asking ourselves, "What should I do?" only to arrive at third base saying, "I don't know!"

Stop the silliness! He has a plan for you. He spoke

about it in Jeremiah 29:11, when He said that He has plans for you—"plans to prosper you and not to harm you, plans to give you hope and a future." Wouldn't it then make sense that He might want to share it with you?

It's interesting how many people will talk and pray about their goals, dreams, and problems . . . but it seems to me there is less emphasis today on giving God the opportunity to actually respond. To talk back. We may ask God questions, but we seldom give Him the time to answer us. We're too busy or too frantic to be still and listen.

> **Have you ever been praying so hard to God that you didn't take the time to listen to what He had to say on the subject?**

In business it would be a big mistake to have a job where you didn't know the company had a plan for your professional development. We always want to hear that the CEO has a role for us to play in the organization's future, that we're part of the big picture. But when it comes to the question, "Does God have a good plan for me?" even though we all *hope* He does, for some reason we have been deceived into believing that the CEO of the Universe isn't longing to sit down with us daily and tell us. I can tell you from experience, He does want to tell you.

In Proverbs 16:1, God says, "To humans belong the

plans of the heart, but from the LORD comes the proper answer of the tongue" (NIV). I love this because just like my mom and dad loved to give me advice on my goals, dreams, or problems I faced, God Himself has a reply He wants to give you on your situation. Have you expressed yours to Him and then listened for His reply? Believe me, He has one specifically for you. And knowing this should so intrigue you that you want to hear more. Let's do that together.

2

OUR STEPS ARE ORDERED

"The steps of a good man are ordered."

PSALM 37:23 KJV

O ne of the reasons I love those three simple but disruptive questions is that they clearly remind us of our need for a "vital connection" with God. Getting to *2 Chairs* was a life-changing moment for me, and I know it will be for you too. But there's more! Once you meet with God, you'll discover something amazing. You'll find out He does more than just listen to you; He has a plan—plans to prosper you, give you hope, and always shed light on your great future.

But to know these plans you have to stop and listen

for His still, small voice in the midst of your troubles. I hope you know that God is aware of what's going on and is capable of helping you through it to accomplish His plans for you, but do you know He also wants to talk to you? That's why I tell people to remember the 80/20 rule at *2 Chairs*: You get to talk for one minute; God gets to talk for four. Or you get two minutes and He gets eight. If you ask God to reveal His plan for you, He will. But trust me, most of the time He doesn't give it to you all at once. More likely He will give it to you day by day, because you couldn't handle it all at once. It would be too wonderful, even a bit unbelievable! Now some haven't yet responded to God's call, but He reminds us in Proverbs 1:23, "If you had responded to my rebuke, I would have poured out my heart to you and made my thoughts known to you."

As I look back on my life I can clearly see His footprints along the way. And I discovered some specific steps He wanted me to follow. As you go through each of these steps, I believe you'll find He has been talking to you about them for years.

Let me show you what I discovered.

Growing up playing team sports was a really great learning experience for me, both in business and in life. I quickly discovered that discipline wasn't just something that was going to be required by Mom and Dad. No, being able to listen, follow orders, and humble myself to others such as coaches, teachers, mentors, employers, or investors was going to be a lifelong test.

How did team sports teach me this? Well, right off the bat, I had to go to practices—lots of them!—and my coaches constantly emphasized being on time and always listening to their instructions on what to do next. When I didn't listen, I would usually find myself running in the wrong direction or, worse, bumping into somebody else on my team. I'm here to tell you that you have to do this only once or twice in front of your teammates, peers, and those you love to never want to do it again.

I also learned that it was really important to be ready when I was called, which meant I had to be prepared. And to be prepared, it was vital that I knew what it actually meant to "be ready." Any resistance to, or rebellion against, those giving me instructions, advice, guidance, or thoughts on necessary changes was seen as immature or prideful. That *never* worked and would only keep me sidelined or riding the bench. And I can tell you from personal experience that when I didn't stay focused on the football field or basketball court, there was an immediate response from the coach. "Beaudine, weren't you listening?" It took running laps before I came to my senses and figured out that following orders and listening was a much better idea.

Being ready encompasses things like vision, desire, preparation, and patience because you never know when your number will be called. In sports, coaches clearly see the difference between the unengaged and the engaged players. The first group just hangs out at the water cooler joking around. Most of them probably couldn't even tell you the score. But those players who watch the game, are aware of every situation, and those who stand close to the coach show character, respect, and maturity. And those are the players who are more likely to get into the game. Just as in sports, you'll miss out on the action in life—all that God intends for you—if you are not ready.

> **Being ready encompasses things like vision, desire, preparation, and patience because you never know when your number will be called.**

In life there are great benefits to listening and being ready, and this idea of being ready is not an every-once-in-a-while concept; no, it's a daily choice . . . so how we start our day matters. When you allow others to teach, mentor, and manage you, you are seen as a person with great leadership capability. On the other hand, if you don't listen, aren't ready for opportunities when they arise, and are unwilling to serve others for a greater good, you will miss out on both big and small successes.

I must tell you that I initially had trouble listening to God during my *2 Chairs* moments. I'm sure you will, too, because I think most people do. One of the reasons is that life throws a lot of distractions at us, and when we're not focused on that *one thing* we're supposed to do, confusion settles in and causes even more of a disconnect between our present reality and what God has in store for us. A truth that never changes is this: If you aren't listening to God, who has a plan for your life, someone else will have a plan ready for you.

When my daughter Rachel graduated from San Diego State University, she was like a lot of college graduates today in that she knew more about what she *didn't* want to do than what she *did*. She hadn't been home a full day before she wanted to start interviews and get on to the next stage of her life. But each time she interviewed, God seemed to quickly close the door on that opportunity. Has that ever happened to you—you think you're doing all the right things, but God keeps closing door after door? Rachel had been doing *2 Chairs* for quite some time at this point (she is my daughter after all!) so, of course, she was all the more frustrated and perplexed that God wasn't allowing the next phase of her life to come as easily as she had hoped.

Some people in times of need or trouble like to jump from step one to step three, but I can tell you from experience this doesn't work. You can't move from rookie to All-Star all in one day. It reminds me of when I took accounting in college. One day I skipped class thinking, *No big deal. How much could one class matter?* Well, let me tell you: it mattered a great deal! The next class was a lot more confusing because each class was crucial to the next class if you wanted to get to the right solution. Just like each ordered step has to be taken before we move to the next one.

After several weeks of frustration, Rachel decided she needed to dig in deeper with God. She went to her *2 Chairs* asking, seeking, knocking, and expecting an answer. It's important to note that Rachel likes to do her *2 Chairs* early in the morning, outside during her three- to five-mile run. Along the way she asks God where He wants to sit and talk. And He always says, "How about here at this bench?" or "What about these two fantastic rocks?" or points out another place where they can sit. So during those frustrating and uncertain times, each morning as Rachel and God met to watch the sunrise and talk about her day, it became very clear that God had some things He needed her to do *before* she could move on to the next chapter in life.

This is such a great message for people facing challenges and troubles today. God's timing is not our timing. We live in such a fast-food culture of "give it to me how I want it, when I want it" that we rush past the important things and forget that God has a plan that is better than ours.

The first thing Rachel did, smartly, was start at *2 Chairs*. She then reached out to those closest to her for guidance. I am proud to say that I was one of those people in her inner circle whom she asked for thoughts and strategies, and doing this gave her a better perspective. This led her to do a couple of new things: First, she joined the worship team at church. Rachel is an amazingly gifted singer and always wanted to lead worship but never seemed to have the time. The second thing she did was take an eight-week Dale Carnegie course, which she had always wanted to do—and something I had also done in my twenties. She had to guard against the negative self-talk reminding her that all her friends were starting new jobs and moving to exciting new cities while she was sitting in yet another class. But, to her credit, she focused one day at a time

> We live in such a fast-food culture of "give it to me how I want it, when I want it" that we rush past the important things and forget that God has a plan that is better than ours.

on what God had for her in this season of life—leading worship and attending each Dale Carnegie seminar. She walked confidently in that every day.

Not surprisingly, God's timing turned out to be perfect for Rachel. Both opportunities—being on the worship team and completing the seminar—grew not only her confidence and skill set but, more importantly, deepened her relationship with God. Not too long after graduating from the Dale Carnegie course, previously closed doors were amazingly opened for a great opportunity in the city she wanted to live in most. She went after it with full confidence in God's plan and has been there ever since.

Is it possible God has a plan, some specific steps, that He wants you to follow for your benefit? All throughout my life and the lives of those around me, I have found that He most certainly does. Hindsight makes this so clear. The next seven chapters are steps I hope you will follow, in the order that I have seen God use again and again to bring me and people I know well through the challenges and over the obstacles that are part of daily life.

Step 1: Discover the Secret of *2 Chairs*
Step 2: Call Your *WHO* Friend
Step 3: See the Field
Step 4: Change Will Do You Good
Step 5: Be Strong and Courageous!
Step 6: Order Yourself . . . Eyes Forward
Step 7: "Do the Done"

It all starts at *2 Chairs,* so let's begin!

3

STEP #1
DISCOVER
THE SECRET OF
2 CHAIRS

There is nothing that you could do or think of in life that would be more important than setting this up right now and doing it every day!

—MOM (MARTHA BEAUDINE)

D id you know George Washington talked to God? George Washington, that's right, one of our founding fathers and the first president of the United States. How do we know that? Well, you can actually find it on Mount Vernon's Web site in an article titled "George Washington and Religion." Back in 1776, it seems people overheard him having regular talks with God. Wow! I wonder if it was just as awkward back then as it is today to believe that God Himself would talk to us in our time of need. I bet it was. I heard comedian Lily Tomlin once say, "No one is bothered when you say you talk to God, because that's called 'prayer,' but if you take it a step further and say that God talks to you, well that just might be going overboard and they'll call it 'schizophrenia.'" Since history tells us that personal prayer played an integral part in George Washington's entire life, he obviously believed that talking with God was a key to success. After you read this book, I hope you will too.

I'm sure you'll realize quickly in the story I am about to tell you, that it involved trouble of the highest order for George Washington. Were *2 Chairs* involved? I believe so. George faced great trouble less than six months after signing the Declaration of Independence. He was a general at the time, and due to substantial defeats by the British Army in New York City, his army had dwindled to a few thousand troops from its original thirty thousand strong. Those who remained with George were all-in. Maybe the most telling sign of their devotion was that one-third of his remaining troops did not have boots. Battling frostbite in the month of December, they had to fight with burlap tied around their feet and ankles. He knew, however, that if his forces didn't claim a victory soon, they would be hanged as traitors and the American Revolution would be lost. It is hard to overstate the desperation of that moment for him and his men.

I'm not sure if your current situation looks as bleak but you must do what George Washington most likely did in this moment, since it was already his daily practice: He talked to God! Good decision. I can't tell you how many people try to reason with themselves and others instead of asking God for help. Big mistake! Next, while sitting in the presence of God, Washington adjusted his plans. This is such a big thought. People hate change. But I can promise you that in your worst moments, you will need to make some adjustments. As Washington spent time with the King of kings, he regained his confidence and decided that bold action would be necessary if he and his troops were to win. Just think about that. He was facing the most powerful military the world had ever seen, but in just a few moments with God, Washington's confidence was so renewed that he believed that with God at his side, he could turn this seemingly impossible situation around and win the war.

> I can't tell you how many people try to reason with themselves and others instead of asking God for help. Big mistake!

The plan God gave him involved a surprise attack

on the enemy, who would undoubtedly be sleeping off the previous day's Christmas celebration. The bad part of the plan was that to achieve surprise, they would have to cross an icy river and travel ten miles in the dark and snow, many without boots. To inspire his men for such a moment as this, Washington recited an essay his friend Thomas Paine had written called "The American Crisis," which armed them with something more than weapons; it reminded them of *who* they were, *whose* they were, and the path they were called to follow. The opening line Paine wrote is timeless: "These are the times that try men's souls. I love the man that smiles at trouble, can gather strength from distress, and grow brave by reflection." It was just the spiritual armor they needed.

Armed physically and spiritually, Washington ordered his men "eyes forward" as they crossed the icy river and made the dangerous journey. And it was a good thing he did, because the situation deteriorated pretty quickly. A terrible snowstorm arose and slowed their pre-dawn surprise. Has that happened to you? Just when you thought the worst was over, you get a setback. The cancer returns. Papers are served for divorce. You're indicted. You're fired without cause. Or you're deserted by close friends you thought would be there for you. Well in the midst of increasing obstacles for General Washington and his troops, they never wavered from their commitment. In fact, the snowstorm that delayed their arrival turned out to be a gift from God. The storm was so severe that the enemy decided not to go out in it and never posted a guard that morning.

Washington's army took them by complete surprise hours later. The enemy was described as overwhelmed. Word of the victory spread like wildfire and within months twenty thousand men joined/rejoined Washington's army. Britain's surrender at Yorktown five years later didn't come easy, but I hope you won't forget what made it all possible: George Washington knew exactly where to begin in times of trouble—a *2 Chairs* conversation with God.

You see, God Himself has been seeking relationship with His creation since the beginning of time, wanting our attention, not the other way around. He's calling you right now, even in the midst of all your stuff and your trouble. And He's inviting you, just as He did with my mom and George Washington, into a deep conversation with Him. How do I know that? Well, besides having experienced the transformational effect of *2 Chairs* for nearly forty years myself, God told us in Isaiah 65:24, "Before they call I will answer; while they are still speaking I will hear." And in Psalm 5:3, "In the morning, O LORD, you hear my voice; in the morning I lay my requests before you and wait in expectation." Can you imagine that long before you were even thinking of Him, He's been thinking about you? Even better news is that He has some great and mighty thoughts He'd like to discuss with you about that situation of yours. And He needs some face-to-face time to talk to you about it. The question is, will you take heed to this call and meet with Him at your *2 Chairs*?

Imagine if you were in some big legal trouble and you could sit with Supreme Court Chief Justice John Roberts every morning to discuss your case. Wouldn't you like that? Of course you would! What if you needed to get your personal finances under control and the great Dave Ramsey was knocking on your door each morning to share his secrets of financial peace with you? That would be amazing, wouldn't it? Or how about if you were a recreation league, middle school, or high school basketball coach, and you could start the day by spending thirty minutes with Mike Krzyzewski, Duke University's head basketball coach, to discuss the best way to run a practice or develop leadership, team culture, and a winning program year in and year out? I wouldn't have to twist your arm, would I?

But isn't all of that really nothing compared to the opportunity we've been missing each day? Think about it. What an offer! The idea that the Creator of the universe and the King of kings, God Himself, is waiting to meet with you seems too good to be true. But it is true. Set up your *2 Chairs* and see for yourself. And when you do, I promise you will not be the same.

Now even if we believe this, we can unfortunately take this thought too casually. I have a friend who told me he likes to talk to God in the morning in his bed. He asked me if that's like the *2 Chairs* concept I talk about.

I responded, "If you could have ten minutes every morning with billionaire Warren Buffett to discuss your investment strategy, would you do it?"

He said, "Of course."

"Would you meet with him in your pajamas while you're in your bed?"

My friend laughed and said, "No, I guess I wouldn't. I would set up a special spot in my house where we could talk."

I then asked him one more question. "In your meeting with Mr. Buffett, would you talk about *your* investment strategy the whole time, or would you ask him a few pointed questions and then listen to as much of his advice and wisdom as possible?"

My friend smiled and said, "I get the point."

An intern who worked for us one summer shared with me how he wished he had a relationship with his dad similar to the one I had with mine. I shared with him the *2 Chairs*

> **The idea that God Himself is waiting to meet with you seems too good to be true. But it is true.**

opportunity that day, but he seemed reluctant to accept this concept.

I asked him, "Listen, if there was even a one percent chance that God would meet you tomorrow morning, wouldn't you set up your chairs?"

"Yes! If I really felt He'd come."

I told him that I believed there was a *100* percent chance He would show up! And I reminded him, "If you want something that you've never had, you're going to have to do some things that you've never done."

He said, "Okay, I'll do it."

When he walked into the office the next day, he looked different physically. He seemed much happier, and there was a glow about him that he hadn't brought into the office before. That happens when you meet with God—your countenance changes.

I asked him, "How did it go?"

"I've got to tell you, I felt Him the moment I entered the room and sat down at the *2 Chairs*. It was like nothing ever before! Just sitting there in His presence, everything that was wrong didn't seem so big." He said they talked for over thirty minutes, and that when they finished, he knew he had to get in touch with his dad. "I called and told him how much I loved him, how grateful I was for all he'd done for me." His dad was so moved by the call that he wrote his son a letter of love that next week—a letter the son thought his dad would *never* have written before. *2 Chairs* changed their relationship for the better!

Think about it . . . the chance to come sit with the King, to talk with Him about anything and everything. Even though He knows it all, He still wants you to share the worries, pain, hurt, shame, whatever is going on with you. And when you ask for forgiveness, He forgives, He forgets, and He loves you right where you are. And that's just the beginning of His goodness, because He has so much more for you. He wants to fill you with peace, joy, insight, wisdom, power, and favor beyond anything you could imagine. Each new day, He's designing some specific plans just for you. Even if you were not in immediate trouble, this would be helpful. But how wonderful and amazing His guidance and encouragement is in the most desperate of times.

> Even though He knows it all, He still wants you to share the worries, pain, hurt, shame, whatever is going on with you.

Some will say, "I talk to God," but then describe their talk time as more of a "quiet time" of reading, studying, and doing devotions. And all of that is awesome! I hope you do it more. But that's not really what I'm talking about here. That sounds more like something you'd do in a library, and if someone talked you'd hear *Shh!* What I am asking you to consider is dedicating *2 Chairs* in your house for *real* conversation with God.

For your information, this concept doesn't go back just two hundred years; it goes back *thousands* of years. It's creating a place for "holy ground" in your home, apartment, or wherever you're traveling. Creating a specific place, a strategic one, to go to every day with an expectancy to listen, talk, and understand what God says about your day ahead. But you might be asking, "Why is *2 Chairs* so necessary?" Because this is the beginning and the end, the nucleus of the cell, and the source to your solution. Everything emerges from here. And if you want something right now that you've never had, you're going to have to do some things you've never done. And the first thing God wants is for you to set up your *2 Chairs* so He can talk and share with you.

Now it doesn't matter what kind of chairs you use— whether they're lawn, dining room, living room, or rocking chairs, etc. You don't have to spend money on creating the "just perfect" *2 Chairs* setting. What matters is this: you show up with the expectation to actually speak with *Him*. You don't want to miss this!

Today, we all say we believe in many things, but few truly *believe* in their heart of hearts. We've seen this play out at sporting events year after year. There's always that one team or that one player who *believes*, and even though the situation looks like they're going to lose for sure at the end . . . *BAM!* . . . they do something extraordinary to win. They throw a "Hail Mary" that's caught in the end zone, they hole out from the bunker to win, or they somehow make a ridiculous buzzer-beating winning shot from half court. It's as if they have this built-in belief system they can call upon at any time, something bigger than themselves to propel them to victory. They do! And you have it as well—but first you need to believe in the secret of *2 Chairs.*

One question many folks seem very confused about is such an important one: "Does God actually speak today?" Because if He does, and you *believe* that He does, then what my mom passed on to me is very strategic and timely for you too. It could change everything. In fact, it *will* change everything. For those of you who are in trouble today, have a loved one in trouble, or will experience trouble soon (in others word, everyone!), I suggest you test out this *2 Chairs* concept ASAP!

Some of you may be thinking, *But what about me? I've been in a lot of trouble. How could God want a face-to-face with me when I've had all these continual failures in my life? I'm a mess. What would I have to offer in a conversation like this each day?* That last question is a great one. In fact, it's the pivotal one. What you get to offer is *you.* Nothing is more important to God. In fact, He wants to break bread with you and talk about it all. Now, He didn't say the journey ahead would be easy, nor did He say it would happen overnight. But He did say in the twenty-third Psalm that He would be with you every step of the way.

So now back to our Abbott and Costello routine:

"Does God know your situation?"

"Yes."

"Is it too hard for Him to handle?"

"No."

"Does He have a good plan for you?"

"Yes."

"What is it?"

"I don't know."

"2 Chairs!"

I asked my mom that day in 1976 one final question: "Mom, when the day is over and I did my *2 Chairs* and then went out and did all that I could do, what should I do next?"

She told me, "That's when you'll hear God say, 'See you tomorrow! Same place, same time.'"

God has lots of stories
to share with you about
hardship, rejection, battles,
miracles, and love.
Have you figured out yet that
you're one of His epic stories?
You are not close to done yet.
He wants to tell you that
you're loved, amazing,
fabulous, and special.

4

STEP #2
CALL YOUR *WHO*
FRIEND

You already know everyone you need to know.

—*The Power of WHO!*

There are four words I want you to plant deep in your heart. Never forget them! Especially in times of crisis. What are they? *"You are not alone!"* I know you may feel alone. You may even want to be alone, want to hide, even cry—but that is the exact opposite of what you need to do right now. One of the greatest mistakes people make in times of trouble is that they don't reach out for help and lean on their friends and family in times of need. And this is a big mistake!

All it takes is one thought, one idea, or one great friend that God sends your way to share some compassion, encouragement, direction, and insight to help get you back on track. But this will happen only if you're humble and wise enough to ask, listen, and receive help from those who are near to you, whom God has given to you in times of need. In Ecclesiastes 4:9–10 we are reminded, "Two are better than one, because they have a good return for their work: If one falls down, his friend can help him up. But pity the man who falls and has no one to help him up!" But recognizing who these true friends are from the myriad acquaintances that crowd our life is a difficult task. Why? Because we have not asked God to point out what friends should be in our inner circle. Also, friendship has been redefined in our culture to mean something less than what it actually is. Let me tell you a story.

I'll never forget the lunch. I was just twenty-seven at the time and had been with my dad's executive search firm for less than a year. It was my first business trip to New York with Dad—what a moment! We were calling on one of his favorite clients, *Guideposts* magazine. Lunch was with their founder, the great Norman Vincent Peale. It was like meeting Billy Graham or a United States president. Listening to them banter back and forth, telling stories about changing people's lives for the better, I have to tell you it was awe-inspiring. Just the sound of their voices was fun to listen to. Then all of a sudden, Dr. Peale turned more toward me and started sharing the importance of friendship in life. He said that the development and cultivation of even one friend was of paramount importance. His conversation seemed intentional. It was as if he were passing on a torch to me for a future generation's crisis. Over thirty years have now passed, and the crisis is here.

When did we start calling acquaintances "friends"? When did we start texting our best friends rather than calling them? How can I say we are great friends but we never see each other? A recent Gallup poll reported that men over the age of thirty-five aren't adding new friends as they did when they were younger. They keep their old friends but are not adding new ones. And not only are men over sixty not adding new friends, they're giving up their old ones and focusing on their families. Now, don't get me wrong, focusing on family is always a good thing.

> **When did we start calling acquaintances "friends"? When did we start texting our best friends rather than calling them? How can I say we are great friends but we never see each other?**

But giving up on friends is never a good thing. This is happening not because they want it to but because life has gotten too busy. People all across the globe are talking about this negative trend of having lots of "friends" but no friendships. This, of course, is very disturbing. And people are searching for answers.

When was the last time you had a deep, satisfying conversation with your friend or mate—a time when you truly listened to one another, affirmed one another, and just loved one another? How did you feel? Go ahead and say it—it was awesome! Unfortunately, these moments are becoming rarer by the minute. Once upon a time, building true friendships was one of our goals, what we always said we'd do. Remember BFFs (best friends forever) working together, playing together, and growing old together? Enjoying Saturday barbecues, ball games, campfires, living next door, kids growing up, and going to church together? Doing life with friends. Ahh . . . why do I feel so much better just talking about this? Because outside of having that personal relationship with God—nothing's more important than having a few really close friends you can count on. Without true friends it's hard to survive, let alone thrive.

The friendship crisis that Norman Vincent Peale talked to me about at lunch that day has not only come true but gets significantly worse when troubles cross our paths. Why? Because when trouble hits (and that's what it feels like), the unexpected blow can be overwhelming. The great philosopher Mike Tyson once said, "Everyone has a plan 'til they get hit." And a knockdown like this can take us into unknown territory, disorienting us as we attempt to remain alert and try to acclimate to our new circumstances.

In 2009, I came out with a book called *The Power of WHO!* I couldn't call the book *The Power of Friendship* because we now have thousands of people on social media who are our best "friends." The word *friend* has become somewhat disingenuous, so I created a new word for friends—called your "*WHO*"—the people *WHO* matter most in your life. If you haven't read *The Power of WHO!* then I encourage you to pick up a copy and read it, but for the moment this section will serve as a good summary of the book. I am convinced that God gave you specific people in your life to help you in ways you never imagined and that you already know everyone you need to know.

We all know that trouble lurks all around, but we never expect it to come near us. When you're blindsided by it and lying flat on your back looking up at your adversary or sickness or circumstance, you are surprised, isolated, and discouraged.

- **Surprised** so much that you forget all your common sense.
- **Isolated** and fooled into believing you can do it alone or that you are all alone.

- **Discouraged** and feeling hopeless, where even death thoughts can surface.

So what do you do? Well, in times like these, you need a *WHO* friend. You can't do this alone. You can't get isolated. God has given you specific people for times like this. So immediately call one or more of those friends He has placed on your heart. When you do, you'll find that just talking to them will help you feel better. They will help call a halt to your fearful thinking. They will speak truth about your value and worth, and they will grab hold of you when they see you wandering down the wrong path. They are people who love and care about you, and because they know your true identity, they won't let you forget it. Now listen . . . you might be a genius in some areas, but in times like these you're going to need others to assist you when you're not strong. So please don't attempt to do life on your own. Don't allow yourself to get isolated. More than ever, now is when you need those friends who are willing to take the time and effort to mentor, guide, and assist you in every way they can. We all have these *WHO* friends in our lives, but it is critically important to remember, reach out, and reconnect with them.

Now when I feel low, I love to watch inspirational movies. One of my go-to movies that always supplies me a lift of encouragement is *It's a Wonderful Life* starring

Jimmy Stewart as George Bailey. As you recall from this Christmas classic, George dreams of getting out of his small hometown of Bedford Falls so he can travel the world. After years of working in the family business to save enough money for his trip, trouble hits (surprise!) just as he's about to realize his dream. His father dies and he's presented with a choice: Should he save the savings and loan bank that his dad built or turn it over to his dad's competitor, the evil Mr. Potter? Just as George was faced with this difficult choice, I'm sure you're facing an adversity you never anticipated facing either. Still, moments and choices like these come for everyone at some point in life, if not many times.

George doesn't leave that day to see the world. He stays and builds a wonderful life. He develops friends, has a beautiful wife and family, and does it all with great passion. Things are going well when (surprise!) adversity strikes again when his uncle Billy misplaces a large deposit. When George hears of this, he panics because he knows he may face bankruptcy, fraud charges, and possible jail time. So what does he do? Call his *WHO* friends, right? *Wrong!* No, he goes to the one person (Mr. Potter) who's guaranteed not to help.

We do that when we're surprised, don't we? We go to people in times of trouble who don't really know us, like big-time influencers, acquaintances or, worse, drop-down boxes on social networks. As an executive recruiter I get thousands of resumes each year from people who are looking for new opportunities. Deep down they know that they shouldn't send out unsolicited resumes to people they don't know and who don't know them, but they do it anyway because they feel as though they need to do *something*. And worse, they send them out to: "Dear Sir," "To Whom It May Concern," and "Dear Recruiter." It's crazy and they know it. But they do it anyway.

When trouble comes, why are we often so willing to do anything and everything but reach out to God and our loved ones—those *WHO* are the only ones likely to help us? Because we're humiliated, embarrassed, and don't want our friends and family to know what's happening—even though they probably already know. Pride does that. It prevents us from asking for help from those closest to us. And unfortunately, when we make bad choices, we isolate ourselves and believe the lie that we are all alone. If that's you today—STOP! Run to your *2 Chairs,* and when you're done talking to God Himself, call that special *WHO* friend He gave you. Remember the four words: *you are not alone!*

Now the story of George Bailey thickens. As you probably already surmised, the "evil Mr. Potter" doesn't help him that day. After being spurned, does George wise up and call his close friends/family for help? Unfortunately, no! Instead, George moves rapidly from surprised to isolated to discouraged. I'm sure if you've been in trouble you recognize that these "three" work hand in hand. Well, George gets so depressed that he considers jumping off the nearest bridge. Wow! Is that possible? Would we go so far as to think death thoughts in times like these? Yes, unfortunately many do. And when you look back on your toughest times, I think deep down you can understand exactly what George was experiencing. His back was against the wall. He was in a blind panic, paralyzed with fear and not able to focus on anything but the problem. But luckily for George his closest friend, his wife, Mary, steps in on his behalf and calls his friends all over the city and beyond. They immediately come to help their friend in his time of need.

> When trouble comes, why are we often so willing to do anything and everything but reach out to God and our loved ones—those *WHO* are the only ones likely to help us?

You need to hear this: you are not alone in your crisis either. You've just been thinking incorrectly. That's why calling a *WHO* friend is so important.

Regardless of how awkward or uncomfortable you might feel, just do it! Tell that friend or family member whom God puts on your heart exactly what's going on—the whole truth—and don't leave anything out. Then ask that trusted friend for guidance. Don't be surprised or bothered if there are some people you thought would help you but don't. That's normal. The right ones, the ones whom God Himself has handpicked to help you and mentioned to you at *2 Chairs*, will not only want to help you but are equipped to do so. They will give you the protection, advice, peace, and encouragement you're missing and so much more. And if you will follow this instruction, the one friend God has provided for you here will intercept you on that dark path you're on and redirect your steps back to the path of light. Proverbs 12:25 comes to mind when I think about how a good word from a friend can make all the difference: "An anxious heart weighs a man down, but a kind word cheers him up."

Have you ever noticed that when you share something you really like, such as a great restaurant, a movie, or a great tip, people love to share it with their friends as well? Well, as I started writing *2 Chairs,* I told a few close friends about the life-changing effect I felt the three simple but disruptive questions and seven steps would have on people in their times of trouble. As I shared with them, they agreed and said, "Hurry up with this book. It's going to help a lot of people." I didn't know then how important the three questions would be.

The very next day I got a call from someone I didn't know, who said he had heard from a friend of his that I had written a new book that could be very helpful to him. He asked if he could meet with me to talk about it. I have to tell you, I was kind of shocked having only been writing this new book for a week or so. I told him that when it was done, I'd be happy to meet.

He said, "I hope you don't find this too aggressive, but I can't wait. My twin daughters are seniors in college and suddenly they aren't doing well emotionally." He didn't want to go into it much but said, "One of your great friends told me you have some questions I need to hear. Have you written those down? Could you at least share those with me?"

Hearing the panic in his voice, I said, "Sure."

When we met, I could see he was anxious and didn't want to do the usual casual talk. He wanted to know the three questions. So I jumped in and asked, "Does God know your situation?"

He quickly said, "Yes."

I then asked, "Is this too hard for Him to handle?"

"Of course not!"

I went further: "Does He have a good plan for you?"

I could see the frustration on his face when he said, "I'm sure He does, Bob, but that's the problem, I don't know what the plan is."

61

He spoke about praying long and hard but receiving no answers. I told him God's ways are not always our ways. Sometimes we have to just stop and listen to God. But somehow today, that's become so hard. That's why we all need to start each day at our *2 Chairs*. I also reminded him about Proverbs 15:22, which says, "Plans fail for lack of counsel, but with many advisors they succeed." God so loves each of us that He also has placed friends and specific people across our paths to advise us in times like these. But again, we have to stop and listen and not try to do it all ourselves.

> **"Plans fail for lack of counsel, but with many advisors they succeed."**

Having fathered three daughters myself, I can tell you from personal experience how hard it is not to enable my children and try to provide all the answers for them. I know that so many parents struggle with this too—especially when those children become adults and you don't know where to draw that line between letting them learn how to stand on their own two feet and rescuing them from serious danger. So I asked him, "When your girls were young, did you cut up their food for them?"

He smiled and nodded yes.

"Did you put pretty bows in their hair when they were four or five?"

He glowed for a second while remembering these great times and said, "Absolutely."

You could tell how much he loved his girls. I probed further and asked, "By chance, did you put bows in their hair when they were seventeen?"

He laughed and said, "When they were seventeen, they wouldn't let me touch their hair."

"Don't you think maybe, just maybe, since they're now twenty-one, that you could teach them to have a *2 Chairs* experience for themselves with God? Don't you think he has some things He'd like to tell your girls Himself?"

When I said that, you would have thought a load was just lifted from his back. "That's it!" he said. "I've got to go! I will point them in the right direction rather than do it for them." He sent me an e-mail a couple days later to tell me that the girls loved the idea and how their first couple days at *2 Chairs,* listening to God, changed their entire perspective. It seems they were much more willing to work through their issues with God first, rather than with Dad. I sent him a note back saying how pleased I was and that when I finished writing the book, I would send him and his girls a signed copy.

It wasn't two months later when I heard he'd had a heart attack and died. He was only fifty-six. I was shocked. My mind raced as I thought about how desperate he had been to help his girls, as if time was running out. Did he know? And did God actually orchestrate my sharing the three questions with my friend, so my friend would share with his friend, who would then call me? All that, just so he could share *2 Chairs* with his girls? Wow! I think He did. That's how deeply God cares about us. There's no level of detail He won't arrange to get you to Him.

What a lasting legacy that man left for his daughters. Let me stop here and ask you: Are you listening? Have you heard the call to *2 Chairs*? God has some things to tell you. And then, if you haven't noticed, there are people all around you in trouble who don't know what to do or where to turn. They need for you to help point them in the right direction.

My next-door neighbor Dick had worked successfully in retail management for thirty-plus years when his company changed leadership. He was surprised when he was asked to take an early retirement package, which he did reluctantly. Less than two months later, he discovered that all the golf and traveling he was doing no longer interested him. I could tell one Sunday afternoon that he was a little off his normal chipper attitude, so I asked him to breakfast the next day.

Are you listening? Have you heard the call to *2 Chairs*? God has some things to tell you.

Over coffee, he told me he really missed working,

missed solving problems and helping people. Now, due to his age, he felt that he probably couldn't get a full-time job anymore and was starting to think less of himself. He laughed kind of sarcastically and said, "You know, Bob, there are only so many projects I can do around the house."

I told him, "Dick, you don't have to have a job to help people and solve problems. I am one hundred percent sure God isn't done with you yet." He was intrigued with the thought but needed some encouragement. I suggested he get involved at his local church in their men's group. I reminded him of one of my favorite Zig Ziglar quotes: "If you go out looking for friends, you're going to find they are very scarce. If you go out to be a friend, you'll find them everywhere." The same is true in business.

There is such a great need for mentors and father figures like Dick today, who have a great wealth of wisdom and experience to pass on, but so many times they are waiting for the call. I asked him if he was involved at his church. He told me that he went but hadn't engaged yet. In fact, two young businessmen there had talked about wanting guidance. I said why not call them and say yes. Once he engaged, the word got out, and now he's helping six. In fact, two of them asked him to get involved with advising their company in a paid consulting role.

It's interesting, as I look back over the years, to see how timely some people or certain movies, songs, and great books have been acting as kind of a "message in a bottle" or a "clue" sent to me to get me back on track. That's what happened to Dick, but he needed a friend like me to give him permission to follow his dream. Has that happened to you? I believe when we finally meet God face to face in heaven, we'll find out just how many times God tried to reach out to us but we weren't ready to listen and receive His direction.

Over and over, throughout the years, I have been reminded of just who I am, whose I am, and the path of honor and integrity I am called to walk. But I've also seen in life problems, detours, teachable moments, and lessons I had to learn along the way. Thank God for my *WHO* friends. They are treasures! And without them, I would have been lost so many times. Through these special relationships, I have learned these two vital truths:

1. My greatest allies in times of crises are *the people I already know.*
2. I should never count on *people I don't know* (strangers or mere acquaintances) to help me out of a mess.

You have a network just like one I have. Just like the one George Bailey had but all but forgot about. You have a community of friends that you've built over the years through love and unconditional giving. And they will come to your aid if you just *ask* them. During stressful circumstances, it's easy to forget that our friends are re- sources given to us. That's why it is so important to start with God at our *2 Chairs*. It is there where He will remind you *WHO* He wants you to reach out to. All it takes is one *WHO* friend to help you get a better perspective.

5

STEP #3
SEE THE FIELD

If we could see beyond today . . . we would
not fret, each sorrow we would soon forget.

—NORMAN CLAYTON

On our twenty-fifth wedding anniversary, Cheryl and I went back to Maui, where we'd had our honeymoon. It was a fantastic trip down memory lane. One of the things we did, which we wished we had done as newlyweds years earlier, was drive the "Road to Hana." It's one of the most breathtaking drives on Earth.

Everyone loves this trip—except, of course, if you're the driver of the rental car (me, in this case). I have to tell you, it was no simple feat to accomplish. The fifty-two-mile drive is nerve-racking because it actually has 617 hairpin turns and 56 narrow, one-lane bridges. Seriously, it does! Along the way up to "Heavenly Hana," you see fields of sugarcane, spectacular cliffs, bamboo jungles, waterfalls, and tropical streams. Of course, you never get to see any of those if you're behind the wheel.

I remember Cheryl constantly saying, "Bob, oh my gosh, that's so beautiful," but as I slightly turned my head, she screamed, "No, no, no—don't you look, just drive!"

And I drove and I drove and I drove. And then, finally—whew!—we made it to the town of Hana. Cheryl and I high-fived each other. We then ran over to their store and bought our T-shirts that said, "I Survived the Road to Hana!"

If you think about it, the trouble you face in life is a lot like this "Road to Hana." There are lots of dangerous bridges, hairpin turns, and all-important decisions that must be made right now or, *BAM!*, you're in deep trouble. Wouldn't it be so much easier if you had a traveling companion, a friend who could help guide you through this impossible life you live? Someone who loves you unconditionally, who knows your whole story, and who still has your back? You desperately need that someone who can help get you through this harried journey as safely as possible so you can reach a safe place where you can breathe, reflect, and restore your soul. It is there where you can understand all the issues at hand and make better choices. So, who is this person who can help you in times like these?

Go to your *2 Chairs* and talk to God to see *WHO* He wants you to pick. He has a specific someone for you. In fact, He has probably already given that special someone to you and you just might not have recognized him or her yet. This person is God's key for you. How will you know? Listen to what they say. Listen to how they say it. Great friends speak on a frequency that you will be dialed in to. It's the language of love. In the midst of your toughest moment, your friend will help remind you that you have a hope and a future. This friend will help you carve away those areas in your life that are holding you back.

One of my favorite movies is *The Legend of Bagger Vance,* which describes this situation perfectly. The great young amateur golfer named Rannulph Junuh has lost his true authentic swing, not only in golf but in life. Junuh is playing in a winner-take-all match against two of the greatest names in golf, Bobby Jones and Walter Hagen. On day two of

Wouldn't it be so much easier if you had a traveling companion, a friend who could help guide you through this impossible life you live? Someone who loves you unconditionally, who knows your whole story, and still has your back?

the three-day match, Junuh was down twelve strokes and fighting thoughts of failure, inferiority, and worry about what people would now think about him.

It's then that his caddie, Bagger Vance, declares on the first tee-box, "It's time to see the field."

Junuh sarcastically replies, "I see the field; it's four hundred forty-five yards. It's got a little red flag at the end of it."

We do that in times of trouble, don't we? We let our emotions run roughshod over us. Instead of calming down and talking it over with God at our *2 Chairs* and with that one specific *WHO* friend He gave us, we make the mistake of trying to go it alone and not seeking advice when all looks bleak to us. That's why all of us need a true friend in times of trouble. We need a caddie like Bagger Vance who declares to us, "No! That's not the field. Don't look to the left or the right, don't get impatient, frustrated, or fearful that you're in the woods—just relax. Let me help you. I'll show you the way out."

I was with my dad when they told him he had cancer on the top portion of his right ear. He was stunned. The damage that the sun had inflicted over the years had really done its trick on him. I'm not sure he heard the doctor when he said they needed to surgically take off the top portion of his ear. I think all he heard and felt in his stomach was, *Trouble!* I promise that's not an abnormal response for the various surprises we encounter in life.

After surgery, the doctor smiled and told us that the procedure had been very successful; he felt he got all the cancer. It was not, however, a great thing for my dad, who felt violated and now so very vulnerable with one ear smaller than the other. Dad asked me, "How am I going to go on business development trips with you in the future with an ear looking like this?" We talked about prosthetic ears that day, but after looking at them the next week, it didn't seem right for his specific situation. You could just see his spirit sink that day.

The next week my dad felt even worse. I remember the day vividly when he started talking about "possible retirement."

I said, "No way!" We were sitting at his kitchen table with my mom and my niece Amanda, who was hanging out with her grandpa and grandma that day. Amanda couldn't have been more than six years old at the time.

My dad said, "Bob, listen to me. I look in the mirror and now all I see is three-fourths of the ear. What can I do?"

Then out of the mouths of babes . . . wisdom shouted something so simple. Amanda, who was coloring a picture of a mountain at the time, said, "Papa, why don't you just grow your hair a little longer on the side, and no one would see the difference?"

"What did you say?" we asked.

"Just grow your hair a little longer on the side."

I looked at my dad, and he looked at me. My hair-style at the time was just over my ears. *BAM!* He rushed to the mirror and saw a situation he'd thought was impossible that now was possible. I thought he was going to cry. I think we all did. What a sigh of relief. It wasn't three to four weeks later that Dad's hair was just where he wanted it to be, and no one ever mentioned or noticed his ear again. When you think about it, God definitely has a sense of humor. My dad was literally a Mensa (the highest IQ society) and a nationally respected business executive. Wouldn't it be just like God to use a six-year-old to talk him out of retirement?

Listen—if you're in the midst of a crisis I want to remind you that it's not always easy to see solutions. In fact, the anxiety you're feeling may have you believing that the worst is bound to happen. That's why you need to quickly huddle with that one special friend so you can get some *perspective*. So you can "see the field" correctly.

My dad, in the midst of his storm, could only see an ear that was smaller in size than his other one. There was no apparent solution in sight. And as a result he was thinking of retirement. But did God whisper that simple answer to Amanda that day? I believe He did! And just as God had an answer for my dad that day, He has one for you as well. Go to your *2 Chairs* and see!

One of my great friends and mentors, Ray Davis,

always reminds me in times of trouble of an old hymn he loves, written by Norman Clayton, called "If We Could See Beyond Today."

Old hymns have somehow lost their "coolness" over the years, and now the current generation doesn't even know they exist. That's so sad, because the words and messages in theses hymns that have been passed down from generation to generation are so powerful. When I told Ray I was writing a book on the subject of trouble called *2 Chairs,* he got so excited that he just broke out and recited all three verses of this hymn and did it all by heart. Just listening to him go through it verse by verse was so impactful to me. It gave me such renewed hope. I'm sure he learned these verses in his times of crisis. I loved these lines: "We cannot see what lies before / And so we cling to Him the more."

The older I've become the more appreciative I have become of how God strategically has given me friends and mentors like Ray Davis, who remind me in tough times that *God* knows my tomorrows—so I don't have to. Thank goodness God puts a veil up to protect me. Because if I ever knew the trouble I would face, I'm sure I would miss the blessings of today by worrying, and then I would stop trusting and clinging to Him for my tomorrows.

When trouble and heartache surprise you in life, it's not uncommon to want to head to higher ground for answers. But this isn't always easy with all the distractions and clamor that surround situations like these. What I've learned at *2 Chairs* is that "seeing the field" from God's perspective isn't just for the hard times but for *all* times of our lives. It's so comforting to know that every day God has thoughts He'd like to share with us about friends, family, relationships, career, health, finances, and everything in between.

In 2000, my dad was rushed to the hospital. The lung cancer we thought he had beaten in his last bout years earlier, had spread to his liver. Him being "Super Dad," it never crossed my mind that he could die. In his last few days, we sat and talked as usual about God, family, sports, and life. One morning, he said out of nowhere: "When you finish writing your *fifth* book, I believe you will have accomplished some things that will have a lasting effect on people."

It's so comforting to know that every day God has thoughts He'd like to share with us about friends, family, relationships, career, health, finances, and everything in between.

I was stunned. I thought to myself, *Fifth book?* Where was that coming from? Up until that moment, my dad and I had never discussed the possibility of my ever writing *one* book. No, he was the writer in the family, not me. He contributed a regular column for the *Wall Street Journal* and several years back had written a great book, *Ultimate Success*, for which his friend Josh McDowell had written the foreword. So when I responded to him, I think I laughed out loud and said, "Dad, are you kidding? I can't write a memo!"

He said, "Sure you can. You write extremely well. But the message you have, Bob, is so much bigger than you're thinking; this one, and the ones to come, will change lives. It's time to start writing."

As I look back over my career, I see that I have had opportunities to interview the best of the best in my executive search practice. Hall of Fame coaches, CEOs/titans of industry, studio heads, generals, governors, senators, and even a president of the United States. What's interesting is that there were always two things they all had in common:

1. They all believed they had an assignment, a purpose, a destiny all their own.
2. Each person could tell me about that "one person" with whom they connected along the way, who elevated their perspective as to what they were truly capable of doing. And when they did, their life was never the same.

My dad tried to do that for me that morning, but with all the distractions of the nurses and doctors, and my anxiety of my dad being in the hospital, none of his elevated perspective registered with me.

About a year later, I was helping a friend of a friend who had been let go from his job. He told me he had been out of work for six months and wasn't getting the results he thought he would through cold calls. I said, "Well, of course you're not; networking as we know it today is not working." Then for the next thirty minutes, I led him through the strategy I had been helping others with for years. It was the complete opposite of how networking has been taught over the years.

It wasn't a week or so before he found a better job. He called to thank me and then just blurted out, "Bob, I don't know if you've ever heard this before, but you need to write a book. The strategy you shared with me that day needs to be in bookstores across the country, across the globe." Then he said something that caught me off guard: "A book like this would help so many people, it would change lives." *BAM!* It was then, in a moment's flash, I remembered my conversation with my dad a year prior.

Has someone been trying to get you to elevate your perspective recently? A friend, parent, or coworker in whom you've been confiding? Sometimes it takes another person to see something in you that you can't see yourself—one who is able to speak it to you in a way that enables you to see it too.

You cannot "see the field" correctly on your own. That's why this chapter is placed strategically here. You and I both know that much of life is not as it seems. Take, for instance, your last argument with your spouse about the dishes—it wasn't about the dishes, was it? Or your boss, who always seems angry—the real problem probably has nothing to do with you. Or your daughter whose grades are slipping—maybe she is embarrassed to tell you about something.

> If you're open to God changing your current perspective to *His* perspective, get ready for a wild ride.

Most of our problems are so simple in hindsight. But don't worry. God is all-knowing, and He owns the future, so sitting in *2 Chairs* daily with Him gives us a perspective now that we could not have seen for months or years, if ever. Such a big thought can start only with God!

If you're open to God changing your current perspective to *His* perspective, get ready for a wild ride—the Road to Hana is nothing compared to the one God wants to take you on. And when you see life through God's eyes, you'll be amazed at what opportunities you see.

6

STEP #4
CHANGE WILL
DO YOU GOOD

Is there one decision you could make today that'll make tomorrow better?

—ZIG ZIGLAR

O ne of my heroes growing up was Zig Ziglar. When he'd speak to large groups, he'd always ask two great questions: First, "Is there one decision you could make today that would make tomorrow worse?" The crowd always laughed kind of sheepishly and gave a resounding "Yes!" Then he'd ask, "Is there one decision or *change* you could make today that'll make tomorrow better?" This was interesting, because even though most of the crowd knew they could make better choices, they usually went silent with this question because Zig added the one word, *change.* The idea of change makes most people squirm. But unexpected change that is a result of trouble can be overwhelming. When this occurs, you need to immediately hit the pause button in life and go to your *2 Chairs* to talk to God, remember the people He gave to assist you, see the field, and then make the necessary adjustments.

What if you sit in your *2 Chairs* with God tomorrow and ask Him a few Zig Ziglar–type questions like:

"God, is there one thing that You would like me to change today? What about an attitude change You'd like me to make, such as being more positive with people or more humble? Maybe it's a matter of the heart where I've closed off some people or am not forgiving them?" (As you're asking these questions, listen for what God is telling you.)

What if you went further and asked God about stopping self-destructive behaviors such as overdrinking, anger, being critical of others, always being late, or maybe self-pity/bitterness? (What is He telling you?)

What if you asked Him about that one action step He wants you to take today, like learning a new skill, being a better friend, mentoring a young kid, or even starting an exercise program several times a week to feel better? (What did God say?)

What's amazing is that when you set up your *2 Chairs* and start a simple dialogue with God like this, He actually speaks back. In fact, don't do *2 Chairs* if you really don't want God to talk, because He *will* talk. Why? Well, for no other reason than He loves you. And He wants you to know it. You're His son, His daughter, and there's nothing more important to Him than spending time with you. He has so much He wants to share.

My dad mirrored this concept for me growing up. When he got home from work, he would always change from his work clothes and put on his jeans, sweatshirt, and ball cap. He knew how important it was to take off all the concerns from work when he got home, and changing clothes helped him focus on family. We would then grab some baseball gloves and throw the ball out in the front yard. I have to tell you that this was such a great time. Watching the movie *Field of Dreams* and seeing Kevin Costner's character ask his dad to play catch, I always tear up, because it reminds me of those times with my dad throwing the ball, talking about our day, laughing, and telling stories. It's in simple times like these, talking through

> **Don't do *2 Chairs* if you really don't want God to talk, because He *will* talk. Why? Well, for no other reason than He loves you. And He wants you to know it.**

life with our parents, that we get our sense of identity.

I did the same with my girls—Aly, Jenny, and Rachel—as they grew up. Each time we went out to kick the soccer ball, bump volleyballs, or play catch after I got home from work, I made sure we also had what I called "download moments." Moments to pass on wisdom and tell stories of tough times that God helped me through when I turned to Him. I learned from my wife, Cheryl, how important it is to make time to just *listen* to my girls. Young fathers need to hear this: Young girls aren't like boys. They need you to listen to them. Listening builds their self-esteem. From my experience with my three amazing daughters, I promise that if you will make time to listen, it will pay great dividends as years go on. Don't forget, always finish by giving them a hug and telling them how proud you are of them. And make sure you tell your daughters that they're beautiful . . . or someone else will!

Did you know God loves to have moments like these with you? He yearns to talk, laugh, listen, and share. If you didn't know it, He's got lots of stories to share with you about hardship, rejection, battles, miracles, and love. Have you figured out yet that you're one of His epic stories? You are not close to done yet, but He wants to tell you that you're loved, amazing, fabulous, and special. He wants you to know that as His beloved child, you are a person of infinite worth, of royal descent, and the object of His affection. When you're at your *2 Chairs*, ask Him to help you understand this more. Then remind yourself to also read some of God's greatest stories in the Bible. I've heard so many people say that while they were at *2 Chairs* praying, talking to God, they felt led to open the Bible. And when they did, God wouldn't stop talking.

I recently explained the *2 Chairs* concept to my friend Bill, who was going through a really tough time. Given his unhappy state of mind, it was no surprise that he set up his *2 Chairs* the very next day. He was still in shock when he described his first meeting. "It was wonderful," he said. "It was as if God hugged me the whole time." So many people get that same type of love fest in their first *2 Chairs* meeting. Up until then, my friend had thought God was mad at him, but now he knows better. The very next day he woke up late and was rushing off to work when he looked back at his *2 Chairs* and felt God saying, "Bill, don't leave before we talk. I want to tell you something about the day ahead." Since the idea of talking to God was new to him, he thought, *Hey, am I saying that to myself? Because I just don't have time today!* That's when he felt the nudge to go back and sit down, so he did. He told me that he'll never forget what happened next.

As soon as he sat down, God started speaking. Now Bill wanted to make sure he told me he didn't hear God audibly, but he could hear Him speak clearly in his mind nevertheless. When you first start doing *2 Chairs* you don't know what it will be like. Yes, He can talk audibly—He's God! But most know how the enemy speaks clearly in their mind, so for Bill, hearing God turn this in a positive way was very comforting. God told him to prepare for some resistance on the important business proposal he was making just before lunch, and that he should make sure to stop by the big boss's office first to review the presentation and ask him for his ideas and suggestions before the meeting. That was it. Sixty seconds. And then he felt the meeting was over.

Now hearing a message from God that his proposal would be met with resistance was not what Bill was expecting, and it was bothersome since he is not someone who likes *change*. He had been working on this project for over six months, and in addition to that, he hadn't talked to the president for several weeks and felt stopping by unannounced might be awkward. But he did it anyway. The president was glad to see him. They talked about family, and then he asked Bill how things were going. Bill told him that his big presentation was at lunch and wondered if he could get some thoughts on it. The president said of course, and as he listened, he guided Bill toward one point that was actually the key for the upcoming year. He said not to talk about anything else but to focus on that, and to tell everyone else why it was so important. Bill thanked him and then changed his entire presentation in the next three hours to laser-focus on this one point.

When the meeting began, Bill immediately felt resistance from two of his colleagues—the two whom he had been confiding in on this project. He couldn't believe it. He thought to himself, *Holy cow! It's true; God knew!* As he started to share the new version of the presentation, the president of the company stopped in to listen. Everyone in the room noticed when he entered. When Bill shared the *one point* that was key to the company, from the back of the room, the president said, "That sounds like a winner, Bill!" and gave Bill's boss a thumbs-up as he left the room. Bill's manager then stated that it was an idea that was well thought out and that the project was a go. Bill walked out of the meeting thinking to himself, *What just happened? Is it possible that God knew what was ahead for me? And if I would just stop and listen to Him at* 2 Chairs, *that* one minute *could make all the difference?* He proclaimed, "God is a ninja!" And I agreed.

Some changes are much tougher than others, but from my experience at *2 Chairs,* most times God will share thoughts and ideas that are easy to put into action—changes that bring almost immediate results when you make them.

Let me show you an example of what I'm talking about here.

I was recently in Cabo San Lucas on vacation with two of our great *WHO* friends, George and Ruth Brandon. One day we decided to play golf at a new, fantastic Jack Nicklaus–designed course right on the ocean called Quivira Golf Club. It has breathtaking views. Now George doesn't play a lot of golf but loves the game and actually could be a really good golfer if he put some effort into practicing more. Unfortunately for all of us who play the game of golf, when you don't practice or play a lot, all it takes is one slight flaw in your swing to cause your whole day to be a disaster.

When I saw George setting up his first drive of the day, I could tell he was aiming pretty far left to compensate for a slice. The problem is that a slice takes out most of the power and distance of a drive. And when he hit it, it was a typical banana ball that went about 210 yards and landed in the right rough. I played a lot of golf growing up, but I didn't want to be a know-it-all giving corrections on the first tee, so I kept my mouth shut. On the second tee, George hit another slice, and I could see by his reaction that he was disappointed and he had hoped for a better result. At this point, I couldn't help myself. I asked him if I could make one simple suggestion, and he said yes. We teed up another ball and this time I set him up to aim down the left-hand side of the fairway. I told him all he needed to do was pull his right shoulder back, as if his shoulders would point in the direction he wanted the ball to go. "That's it!" I told him this one simple change would be all he needed to get his clubface back to square on impact. I then said, "Just let it rip." He crushed it right down the middle, over 300 yards! He was stunned. One slight change and after that he hit the next twelve fairways dead-center. All were crushing blows of 280 to 310 yards in distance. To say he was excited would be an understatement.

That's what happens sometimes at *2 Chairs*. You sit with God, and He suggests a few small changes in your life—not big, crazy, impossible ones. He might tell you that there are a few people who are not good for you to hang around with any longer or point out some television channels that aren't good for you to watch and suggest some alternatives that will make you feel much better. And if you're not feeling healthy and happy about the way you look, don't be surprised if He suggests you get some exercise and eat a few more fruits, vegetables, and salads. This could sound too simple, but we all know small changes make big differences.

On the other hand, unfortunately some problems require bigger actions because you've overlooked them for some time now. Issues like:

- You never thought your mate would actually file for divorce even though the two of you have been

'ng for years and you haven't been paying at-
.ntion to your spouse.

- You *suddenly* have a heart attack, but your family
  has a history of heart attacks—and you're over-
  weight, don't exercise, and have been pressing too
  hard for too long.
- You can't believe they let you go at work even
  though you've hated your job and let everyone
  know about it.

Many people wake up and find themselves in this position and are totally caught off guard. But thank goodness
that when we're overwhelmed, God isn't. And yes, even
now, in your worst moment, He still has your back. It's
here that you need to ask the three simple but disruptive
questions.

1. Does God know your situation? *YES!*
2. Is it too hard for Him to handle? *NO!*
3. Does He have a good plan for you? *YES!*

So what do you do? Run to your *2 Chairs* and ask Him.
Just by showing up at *2 Chairs* you will have found your
way to the right place. You will be exactly where He wants
you to be—with *Him*. And don't worry, whatever changes
He deems necessary, I can promise you two things: They
won't be complicated, and they will do you good. Let me

tell you about a small change that I had to make in my life that many will also need to make, if they're to fully enjoy the blessings of *2 Chairs*.

As we all know, going to dinner at restaurants with kids can be very stressful for parents. But growing up as a Beaudine, I found it was always a fun-filled event with many amazing conversations. People who sat nearby us were so amazed that they would come by the table after dinner and remark to my parents how well-behaved we were. And that was before there were iPods, iPhones, or handheld video games to entertain us.

My dad accomplished this feat by creating an ingenious game called "Penny, Nickel, Dime." The concept of the game was that Dad would ask questions to each of us, one at a time. Each child could decide what level of question he or she wanted. A penny question was fairly easy, a nickel choice was more challenging, and a dime . . . well, that was flat-out tough. You had five categories to choose from: current events, sports, US presidents, family history, or the Bible. Dad made up all the questions. Each time it went around you got a different question from a different category. It was surprising how much you learned at dinner. We never got bored with the game. But the small change my dad put in place when going out to dinner was the antidote to the normal kid arguments and fights parents usually had to manage.

Later in life, my dad continued these great dinner

conversations with me as we traveled together in business. But instead of conducting contests, he made them more like teaching moments, instilling in me core values that would last a lifetime. He'd ask questions about my most embarrassing moment, my greatest highs, greatest lows, etc. He would always share his as well. One conversation I'll never forget was at one of Dad's favorite restaurants, The Bull and the Bear at the Waldorf Astoria hotel in New York. This particular night he presented a scenario and asked a couple of questions that moved me.

"Bob, what if we had an argument one day at work that was silly, but it escalated and I said a lot of things that were not nice or true, and you were hurt? And worse, what if I was caught in the trap of being so embarrassed or prideful that I couldn't call you or come over later and say I was sorry? Here's my question: Would you be man enough to call me or come over to my house and tell me you were sorry—even if you weren't in the wrong—and unlock me from the trap I was in?"

I looked at my dad and said, "Wow, that's a heavy question. Let me say this, Dad, I hope and pray I would be man enough."

Well, it wasn't three months later when we had a silly argument that escalated. Now, the older I get the more I see that *all* arguments are silly . . . but even back then I should have recognized that my dad was tired from being gone on a long trip. He had lots on his mind, and when our disagreement worsened, he said a bunch of stuff I knew he didn't mean, but it still hurt me. Of course, it wasn't as if I hadn't also said a few things that hurt him, but he was clearly out of line. Now in our family I was always taught growing up: "Don't let the sun go down on your wrath." In other words, someone before the night ends always has to be a big enough person to say they are sorry.

When 9:00 p.m. came around, I was very concerned that my dad hadn't called to apologize. That's when I clearly heard something within me ask, "Are you man enough?" I knew exactly what that meant and what I had to do. I told Cheryl I'd be back in a few minutes and got in my car and drove over to his house. My parents only lived a few blocks away. I knocked on the door and he answered. He looked sad. He looked fatigued, and his shoulders were slumped forward. Being unable or unwilling to forgive does that to all of us in times like these. It just drains all the life and energy from us.

I spoke first, "Dad, I'm so sorry." I wanted to say more, but before I could, he suddenly broke out in tears, put his arms around me, and hugged me so hard.

"No, I'm sorry," he said. "I so appreciate your coming over here tonight." And then he looked at me and said, "I'm free!"

I'll never forget that moment. The memory makes

me tear up. It inspires me to tell you: PLEASE don't let an unforgiving heart hold you or your loved ones hostage even one minute longer. If there's something in your past that is hindering what was once a close relationship, clear it up now. Say you're sorry first. It's a change that will do you good!

Maybe you're a person who looks as though you have everything going for yourself, but if we'd dig a little deeper we'd see that something is missing. My daughter Jenny's life should have been "over-the-top great" as she was happily married, the mother of an eighteen-month-old daughter, Emma (the cutest), and she and her husband, Rob, had just bought their first home. But Jenny was miserable.

A high school teacher in journalism/yearbook, Jenny found that from their new home, it now took her over an hour to drive to and from work each day. That meant getting up extra early, getting Emma to daycare, and fighting traffic and feelings of guilt over being away from her. She also put a lot of pressure on herself to be a great wife and supermom. She tried her best to fight off the negative thoughts for a while, but slowly during her daily commutes, the frustration of it all became an obstacle in her life.

Now I have to tell you that Jenny has always been upbeat her whole life, pretty much amazing at most everything she tackled. So seeing her frustrated and depressed was alarming. She decided quickly she needed a new teaching opportunity closer to home. But teaching roles in the area of journalism weren't easy to obtain. Most schools only have one journalism teacher, and teachers who have those jobs don't often leave.

When the first interview opportunity arose, she wanted the teaching position badly. The only problem was that when she walked in, everyone in the room could sense all the frustration she was feeling. When you want something or someone too much, you can end up sabotaging yourself. Now this is a great tip for you to know! All people carry with them their own unique "presence" that is invisibly transmitted to everyone around them. When you walk into a room, you want to make sure you bring your best, most positively charged attitude.

> **All people carry with them their own unique "presence" that is invisibly transmitted to everyone around them. When you walk into a room, you want to make sure you bring your best, most positively charged attitude.**

And it has to be genuine because people can tell the difference immediately! That day, Jenny just didn't have it. After hearing someone else got the job, she was heartbroken.

It wasn't a week later when Jenny called and said, "Dad,

I need some advice." I told Jenny about this *2 Chairs* book that I was working on and said there were two specific things from what I was writing that I thought would be invaluable for her in her crisis. The first was reminding her to go back to her *2 Chairs*. Go talk to God—nothing goes before that. This was something she already knew, but the busyness of life had gotten the best of her. And anytime she could be at her *2 Chairs,* there she would find wisdom, peace, and—even better—her Best Friend!

But the second thing I felt would help her was related to her words. They were uncharacteristically negative. I told her that a small change would do her good. Whatever messages she was hearing from her self-talk, television shows, or others she was associating with weren't helping her. I had a suggestion, a remedy for this problem. But I told her it would require a couple of changes. And this isn't always easy. I told her a tip that had worked for me over the years: when the pain of not having what you want is greater than the pain of change, you'll take action.

I asked her if she had Sirius radio in her car, and she said yes. I told her to check out Joel Osteen's channel, which offers positive inspiration for life. If she would just do the *2 Chairs* and then listen to uplifting messages while driving to and from school every day for the next month, this small change could make a big difference. It wasn't even two weeks later when I started hearing changes in

Jenny's voice. She was bubbling over, now talking optimistically about herself, her situation, and her future.

Wow! Just two weeks later, and out of nowhere, she was called to interview at the specific school district of her dreams, which was close to her home.

Jenny's interview went amazingly well that day. She said it was so positive. She said, "I was so calm, so confident, Dad, that I felt there was favor in the room for me even before I entered." She got the job! The principal remarked after the interview, that a big reason she got the job over the many other candidates who interviewed was because of how positive she was.

Did Jenny's circumstances change before she got the interview? No! The long drive was still there, the frustrations, the pressures of being a wife and mom—all that was still the same. What changed? Maybe, just maybe, it had to do with the change in Jenny's attitude. And this came by choosing to fill up each morning at *2 Chairs* and then using the time in her car more effectively and getting inspired by stories of God's promises, His faithfulness, and His comeback power.

Maybe for you it's reading inspiring books, listening to the right music, joining an exercise club, or eliminating negative television consumption. I can tell you as a dad, I was so proud of Jenny's foresight in recognizing a problem and taking action. I can't tell you how many times I have seen someone allow a problem to escalate over time, making the solution much more difficult and taking its toll on the person.

As you look back on this chapter, you'll see I didn't choose to tell you tough stories about someone losing 150 pounds or getting their life back after prison. And for good reason. I have several of those stories—and they are awesome—but the stories I chose to share all have one thing in common. They started with *one change* that was small and doable:

- Talking/listening to God before an important business meeting.
- Making a small adjustment with your shoulders on your golf swing.
- Filling your mind with inspiration on your commute to work.

Small, doable changes that, when made a habit, snowballed into a bigger change.

So, how do you begin? Simple. This all starts when you decide to make *2 Chairs* with God a habit every morning. The world will allow problems to consume you, but God knows that *change will do you good*, and He's there each morning to talk it through with you. If you will stick with the *2 Chairs* meetings you've been having and the minor adjustments you have made, then you will begin to experience success and peace, compounded week after week, month after month, and year after year. Before you know it, and seemingly all of a sudden, you'll realize that you have this amazing testimony of how God has brought you from where you were to where you are.

One quick warning before we go to the next chapter: Since God sees the beginning and the end, He knows your opponent will not be pleased that you are spending time with Him at *2 Chairs* and are trying to make some real positive changes in your life. As a result, you can expect an all-out fight to get you back to where you were. But don't be too concerned, because God will provide the strength and courage you need just for such times as these.

Psalm 32:8 says,
"I will instruct you
and teach you in the way
you should go;
I will counsel you
and watch over you."
Wow! Can you imagine
that God Himself is
personally going to instruct,
teach, and guide you?

7

STEP #5
BE STRONG AND
COURAGEOUS!

God will be with you wherever you go.

—*Joshua 1:9*

My favorite scenes in the James Bond movies are when 007 gets together with his old friend "Q," played by Desmond Llewelyn. Do you remember him? His character is the inventor of all the cool gadgets 007 gets to use to withstand the evil he faces. Gadgets like special ring cameras, umbrellas that are flame throwers, as well as shoes, hats, watches, and briefcases that are each designed to save the day. The cars he drives have ejector seats or can even turn into a submarine! I always look forward to the next Bond movie to see what new gadgets will be invented next! I think we love these scenes because deep down we wish that surviving life's battles was as easy as having the right gadget.

Unfortunately, the obstacles that life continues to throw at us aren't remedied by worldly gadgets. It's going to take real strength and courage to face these difficulties head-on. But wouldn't it be like God to have a simple answer that is better than anything we have? I've got some good news for you—He does! In fact, it's so simple that it is just one word—*relationship*—going deeper with Him. Life never seems to get easier, but we can know God more today than yesterday, and more tomorrow than today. When we do, He will transmit to us more strength and courage than we could ever imagine, because His supply is limitless.

I'll never forget the day my dad had someone in his office when I barged in as I always did, only to find he was meeting that morning with Ross Perot Sr. Mr. Perot was a very successful businessman in Dallas, having founded EDS in 1962, selling it to General Motors in 1984 before starting Perot Systems in 1988. But he was probably best known for being an independent US presidential candidate in 1992.

I apologized for the interruption, but my dad jumped up, excited to introduce me to Ross. Introductions by my dad were always over the top, fantastic. He always acted so proud to introduce his family. It made me feel alive! It reminded me who I was—his son. Mr. Perot couldn't have been nicer that day. He loved that I was in the family business, just as his son was. We talked about everything that morning from business to politics to our country. But the overriding conversation was the importance of identity and the crucial role each father plays in affirming a positive self-image for each of his children.

I've watched other fathers in similar situations, who unfortunately have missed opportunities to affirm their children. What were they thinking? Given the same chance that morning, my dad chose to celebrate me and not be bothered by the interruption. He never missed an opportunity to instill confidence in me to walk boldly in my position as his son toward my goals and dreams.

I was clearly blessed to be a son of Frank Beaudine. I found out quickly that meant something big when I joined my dad's company, Eastman & Beaudine. Because of who he was and how he lived his life, I was given something freely that others weren't because of the price he paid forward to me. I can only describe it as *unmerited favor*. Those who were Dad's friends and clients always greeted me with endearing love and a strong confidence that I would follow in his footsteps. Now, I understood this wouldn't last if I didn't walk in a similar manner, but I never took this lightly, and as a result I've been blessed.

Many of you who are reading this didn't have an opportunity to grow up with a dad like mine. But don't let that concern you, because you've been made in God's image. You are God's son. You are God's daughter. This is infinitely better, and knowing this changes everything and is the source of your strength. Sitting with God at *2 Chairs* every morning is your daily reminder of this. I've always tried to model that for my family as my dad did for us. I always try to remind my children that they are covered, I have their back, and nothing they do can change that. God feels that way about you too—exponentially. The more time you spend with Him and the more you listen to Him, the more confident you will be that life's battles aren't yours to fight but His.

When people ask me what it's like to sit at *2 Chairs*, I jokingly advise them to make sure they install seat belts. Because there is no preparation for an encounter like this. Brace yourself. Why? Because God knows your name, He wants you to sit with Him, and when anyone asks Him about you, He tells them you are His.

He's waiting to meet with you each day at *2 Chairs* to discuss all that's on your mind—the good, the bad, and the ugly. This is infinitely better than just a relationship with an earthly dad. But to give you more ammunition, as a CEO of an executive search firm, I am trained to look at and discern resumes and backgrounds. I've seen God's resume and all His accomplishments, and I must tell you they're *really, really* good. For your information, He always succeeds, always wins, and has no lack of resources. In fact, no weapon formed against Him can prevail. So in times of trouble, having Him on your side is a very good idea. But you have a part here to play! He is asking you to re-linquish your problems to Him in return for His strength and courage. Only His strength and courage is battle-tested for every kind of trouble.

It will provide you a covering to withstand the obstacles of the day. He may not always get rid of them, but He will help you withstand them!

You've been made in God's image. You are God's son. You are God's daughter. Knowing this changes everything!

Many don't know about this. Beginning to understand this is a result of going deeper with God, and many miss it. Simply put, some think that the concept of talking to God at *2 Chairs* is just a scheduled appointment to report back or brief God on our daily problems instead of giving them to Him and realizing He is actually in the trenches with us as we go through things. Big mistake! He promises that He will be with us *wherever* we go. But let's delve deeper—why do we need to understand this?

Well, I wish I could tell you that after finishing Chapter

4, "Change Will Do You Good," and having made some much-needed changes and adjustments, your problems would be over. We all know this is not always true. At best, you're still going to have setbacks. More likely, though, when you're in trouble things are going to get worse before they get better. And you're going to need some help! We can't do it alone because our human strength and courage are insufficient. Fortunately, we can take great comfort in knowing that God knows this and has promised to walk through it with us. In fact, He designed it this way so difficulty would press us to seek and cling to Him!

We've all tried things our way and know firsthand what it feels like to hear Dr. Phil's line year after year: "How's that working for you?" Well, it's not been working well! Over the years, I have had to learn to submit to God, allowing His strength and courage to be transmitted to me at *2 Chairs*. His strength becomes my strength. His courage, my courage. When this happens, I have the confidence of a favored son and am able to confront any obstacle—and everyone around me can feel it.

I had a chance to go to the White House with my dad during the term of President George H. W. Bush. It was amazing! When we arrived at the White House, I immediately felt a rush of adrenaline and sensed what a special place it is. What an atmosphere they intentionally designed. They had a full military band for our event that night, and there were less than sixty of us invited. The flowers, the tables, and the china created a festival for the eyes. The coolness of being there was beyond imagination. Wherever we went, the White House staff knew exactly who we were, and they celebrated us from the moment they greeted us. What was interesting was that each staff member I met carried with them a "personal environment" of grace and favor because of whom they served. We could sense the "power" they had, and yet because they knew they had it, they never felt the need to laud it over us.

Everyone carries with them what I call a "personal environment." Have you noticed this? When certain people walk into a room, you can *feel* it. They have a confidence and radiance about them others don't. It is clear to everyone that they know exactly who they are. Similarly, you can often tell when there is something wrong with people. Their whole countenance feels negative. Their eyes are tired or sad, their energy level is low, and their body language carries shame, guilt, or worry.

Naturally, we can understand why a president of the United States has a different personal environment than the rest of us—he's the president. But surprisingly, my dad and I were struck by how the staff also had this. Just by working at the White House and serving the president, something fantastic seemed to be transmitted invisibly to each of them. Can you imagine the personal environment you and

I can have transmitted to us at *2 Chairs* by the Creator of the universe when God Himself breathes life, hope, confidence, and perspective into our daily circumstances? This is a game changer! Now we all would agree that working at the White House or in sports or entertainment sounds pretty exciting. But come on, it's not even in the realm of what I am suggesting . . . meeting with God daily.

As my dad and I walked around the White House, we saw firsthand the original paintings on the walls of all the previous presidents, which gave me goose bumps. The picture of John F. Kennedy was incredible. Then my dad and I actually had the opportunity to sit in the two chairs that Ronald Reagan and Mikhail Gorbachev sat in by the fireplace as they cultivated their friendship. We could feel history pulsing through us as we sat in them, imagining the conversations that probably led to the Berlin Wall being torn down.

Then it happened. We were called into a corridor, where the president was going to be announced, and the band began to play "Hail to the Chief." All of a sudden President Bush and First Lady Barbara Bush stepped through a door from their private quarters that was being guarded by two secret service men. As they started walking down the corridor toward us, you could just feel the immensity of the moment! The power, the grace, and the favor of the office of the president of the United States was suddenly transmitted toward us as a surge of energy. It hit all of us in the corridor in a thunderous wave. As they got closer to speak to us, I was overcome with emotion and immediately brought to tears. I looked at my dad to see how this moment was affecting him, and he was tearing up too!

Is that possible? Can people change the atmosphere of a room just by walking into it? It's as if they are wearing a covering around them that projects strength and courage. When you're in their presence, it is impossible not to feel it. Now that might sound kind of crazy, but you and I both know it's true. Anyone who has met a president of the United States, a military general, a Hollywood star, or a big-time athlete has experienced this. But their personal environments pale in comparison to the one that is available to you as God's son or daughter.

> Working at the White House or in sports or entertainment sounds pretty exciting. But come on, it's not even in the realm of what I am suggesting . . . meeting with God daily.

Let's pause for a minute to recap. Life's troubles do not always get immediately better—there will be setbacks and detours ahead. But God wants to remind us daily of three things:

1. We belong to Him, and He couldn't be prouder.
2. His strength and courage are transmitted to us at *2 Chairs*, dramatically changing our personal environment.
3. He is with us wherever we go.

A few years ago during a sleepless night in a New York City hotel room, God showed me that He's with me wherever I go.

When I was writing my first book, *The Power of WHO!*, I never thought it was actually possible to be a guest on a top morning show like the *TODAY* show. Like most people, I had never been on television before, nor had I ever been in a situation where millions of people would be watching me. But, ironically, as I wrote in the book, "All it takes is just one thought, one idea, or one great WHO friend and your world can change for the better in a moment's flash." For me that friend was Jim Hoffman. His recommendation to NBC of both me and *The Power of WHO!* opened a door for one of the most exciting and fearful events of my life. But if I hadn't known about *2 Chairs*, I would have been a basket case.

Cheryl, our girls, and I flew to New York with my trusted friend and PR guru Dennis Welch. We arrived around 4:00 p.m. and had to be at the *TODAY* studio in Rockefeller Center at 7:00 a.m. the next day. We had a quiet dinner and then went back to the hotel early to get a good night's sleep. We had connecting rooms for the girls so they could watch a movie they wanted to see and I could relax. We went to bed around 10:30 p.m., and Cheryl fell asleep pretty quickly.

That's when *fear* stormed into the room. I was just thinking about the show and what I'd say about *The Power of WHO!* when out of nowhere, this thought entered in: *Bob, you're going to be on the TODAY show! You are! And millions will be watching. Think about it. All your friends, family, and clients will be tuned in. In fact, you could ruin the lives of your three daughters, not to mention your entire business, in just four minutes tomorrow if you mess this up.* All of a sudden it was as though I had been hit by Mike Tyson and was down on the mat looking up at the heavyweight champion, not sure what happened.

Has that happened to you? Have you ever heard any of these negative voices when trouble *surprises* you? I'm sure you have. Well, I was going to wake up Cheryl and voice these fears of mine, but I quickly came to my senses and decided to go above her paygrade—*2 Chairs*! I just couldn't allow myself to be overwhelmed by the wave of negative self-talk. I decided I would enter a new, positive thought: *With God's help, I can fight this and win!* But first I needed to change the atmosphere of the room right away, and only the presence of God could do that. I immediately set up *2 Chairs* to intentionally bring God into the room.

Now hotel rooms are interesting places. You don't know who has been there or what has gone on before. So, first, I prayed out loud declaring, "Anything that the enemy had ever done there before, or any lingering negativity still in the room, had to leave immediately." Listen carefully, my friend, our God is a holy God, and honoring His presence in this way is a good thing. The first thing God said as I felt His presence enter the room was that I should turn on some music. God created music to lift, energize, and calm us for moments like these. But more importantly, He transforms our environment in ways that remind us He is there. I grabbed my iPhone and pulled up one of my favorite songs that I listen to in tough times: "Be Still and Know" by Steven Curtis Chapman.

After listening to this song not just once, but over and over for hours, the room's atmosphere changed dramatically from negative to positive. Listen, if you allow tormenting, pestering, negative thoughts to hang around you, they can be disastrous. I chose—and you can too—to turn off that negative self-talk by remembering who I am, Whose I am, and Who is walking with me on the path I'm called to walk. What's your go-to song in tough times like these? If you don't have one, try mine or get one yourself. But put it on your phone so it's there when you need it.

It was now 4:00 a.m., so I decided to shower, shave, and put on my suit. Thirty minutes later I was dressed and standing at the window looking out. It was snowing furiously. As I was listening to a new song by Tracy Lawrence, "Find Out Who Your Friends Are," Cheryl woke up and said, "What are you doing?" I said, "I'm ready." She said, "What do you mean you're ready? It's only four thirty. Have you slept at all?" I said, "No, but it doesn't matter. I'm ready." She sighed, kind of giggled, and went back to sleep.

For the next hour or so I just sat in my *2 Chairs* trying to hear exactly what God's plan was for the show. A couple of hours later, I met Dennis in the lobby, and told him of the battle I had the night before and that I heard God clearly telling me to pray

> I chose—and you can too—to turn off that negative self-talk by remembering who I am, Whose I am, and Who is walking with me on the path I'm called to walk.

with him this morning so that I could get three minutes with Ann Curry before we went on air. I wanted to make sure I could share what *The Power of WHO!* was really all about. Dennis loves to pray and is very bold in times like these. He said, "Father God, You promised if two of us come together and agree on something we ask for, You would help us get it done. We need that help this morning with Ann Curry and that the interview is blessed. Thank You in advance for helping us!"

After arriving at the studio, they sent me to makeup, and then the last twenty minutes was in their famous Green Room with Cheryl and the girls. We hugged, prayed, and enjoyed the crazy moment of being on *TODAY*. Then the producer came in and said, "It's time!" They took me down to the studio and . . . guess what? My interview wouldn't be conducted on the couch in the studio as I thought, but in *two chairs* they set up, one for Ann and one for me. This was clearly a sign.

When Ann turned around and saw me, she said, "Hi, Bob! My dad's name is Bob, I love Bobs!" I thought, *Yes! Fantastic start.* As they were putting on my microphone, one of the assistant directors came over and said, "Three minutes before we go on air, Ann!" Amazing. Just what I had prayed for! Ann then said, "I didn't get a chance to fully read *The Power of WHO!* Tell me about it." I said, "Ann, it's a message of hope. There are millions of people out of a job today, but they won't ask their friends for help because they're humiliated. We could really help people today with this message." Ann said, "I get that, Bob. I covered the tsunami in Thailand, and people there had lost everything but never thought about themselves or asked for help. They'd come up to me and grab my hands, look in my eyes as if they were searching for something. Then, they'd put their hands in a prayer position and bow to me. It happened over and over. I was confused. I asked an interpreter what they were doing. She said that they were looking for God in my eyes, and when they found it they bowed. Wow!"

The director shouted, "Two minutes!" I got a nervous feeling in my stomach. Ann then said, "I saw in the book that you and your dad had a great relationship; tell me about it." I said, "When I was young, my dad was out of work for eight long months. Each day, he'd get dressed in a suit and head to the office. At least that's what I thought he did. When we finally went off to school, he'd circle back home to look for a job. He just couldn't bear for us to be worried; it was a different generation. Years later, when I worked with my dad in executive recruiting, if people ever came to our office looking for a job without an appointment, we'd always treat them as though they had one. We would welcome them to the office and get them a cup of coffee and sit and talk. Dad taught us how lonely and vulnerable it felt to be out of work, and we learned to treat these folks with dignity and compassion. He always told me, 'There's something great in everyone, Bob. It's your job to find it!'"

Ann then said to me, "Listen, we're not going to do the same interview I had planned. This *Power of WHO!* message is awesome. Now remember, Bob, interviews go fast, but don't rush. At the end, I'm going to ask you a question that will tee you up to inspire people who are in trouble. Don't think about it, just let the thought soar into your mind, and when it does—and it will—just deliver it."

Wow! Did she really say that I would get inspiration from above? But on that set in that moment, I believed it. The assistant director shouted, "One minute!" Ann then said something amazing. "Do you mind if I pray for us? I don't consider myself a very religious person, but I'd really like for this to be a great moment for you and this message." She then bowed her head. When she looked up, I said, "Ann, I prayed last night that you'd be my host this morning." She said, "Don't make me cry before we start." The director's countdown began: five, four, three, two . . . and we were on!

What a battle I had fought the night before. But I hadn't been alone. God had given me His strength and courage, and He had walked with me into the unknown adventure. As a result, what an indescribable moment this turned out to be that day. At the end of the show, Ann teed me up as she said she would for one last piece of inspiration. And *BAM!*, out of nowhere God reminded me of a quote by G. K. Chesterton. I told her, "The one thing in life that gives radiance above other things is that there's something great just around the corner! Are you looking for it?" She then said something on-air that was outrageous, "Bob

Beaudine, I just feel good sitting next to you." Wow! What a fantastic thing to say. But I have to tell you as flattering as that was, I can't take credit for the way Ann felt that morning. In reality, the two of us were not sitting alone.

Just as my father had covered me years earlier in a big moment with Ross Perot, God had covered me in a big moment with Ann Curry. Just as the personal environments of White House staff members had been so striking because of whom they served, so too was mine that morning because my first and only goal had been to serve God.

> **The one thing in life that gives radiance above other things is that there's something great just around the corner.**

Just as He has done time and again in my life, and will in yours, God shows up and shows off on my behalf when I start first with Him at *2 Chairs.*

8

STEP #6
ORDER YOURSELF . . .
EYES FORWARD

There are far, far better things ahead than any we leave behind.

—C. S. LEWIS

When you first learn how to drive, parallel parking and backing up are always difficult tasks. The reason is that your rearview mirror is a whole lot smaller than your front windshield. The same is true in times of trouble. It will do you absolutely no good to dwell on the past. You can't get back on the old road. That road has run out. Don't look back! Order yourself . . . eyes forward!

Years back, I loved watching a television show called

Magnum, P.I. with Tom Selleck. There's a great scene I'll never forget as it relates to life's challenges. Magnum is trying to open the door of a Ferrari when two ferocious Dobermans are sprinting toward him, ready to tear him apart. As he struggles to get the key in the door, Magnum screams at the top of his lungs, "Don't look at the dogs! Don't look at the dogs!" Then he glances over his shoulder, only to escape inside the car just in the nick of time. My dad and I loved that scene.

There have been so many times in my life I was either rushing to the airport or late to an important meeting with my dad when we'd hit a snag with unexpected traffic or have to face a huge line at security. I would look at my dad with the same panic in my eyes that Magnum had when he saw the Dobermans, only to hear my dad say, "Don't look at the dogs! Don't look at the dogs!" Then we'd laugh so hard that we brought levity to a tense situation, as well as a new perspective. It was only after a good laugh that I was reminded once again that I don't get to control everything in life. And when I calmed down, things came back into order, lines somehow seemed to move faster, and in the end we usually made the meetings and flights on time. Once again all the worry, tension, and stress turned out to be such a waste of energy.

But don't think that will happen easily and without a fight. Why? Because your enemy, opponent, or negative self-talk is always lurking around waiting for that right moment to either remind you of your past or try to drag you back there. Hear me on this: you *will* be reminded of whatever is in your past that's been problematic or what you've kept hidden. That is, until you order yourself . . . eyes forward!

I've never seen this more clearly than when I've been out on the golf course. I grew up playing golf competitively. So later in life my expectations of my playing skills were far higher than what they should have been given the fact I didn't practice as I did when I was younger.

On Friday afternoons, my dad and I had a routine of playing as many holes of golf as we could play before my mom and my wife, Cheryl, would meet us at the club for dinner. One of the first times we did it, I was really playing well and was shooting even par going into the last two holes when the wheels totally came off my game and I went double bogey, double bogey to finish. Ugh! When we got to the "19th hole" to grab an iced tea, my dad could see that I was not happy. And then he said, "Hey, that four-iron shot you hit on number three

> Your enemy, opponent, or negative self-talk is always lurking around waiting for that right moment to either remind you of your past or try to drag you back there.

was amazing. What did you do there?" After I described the shot, I have to tell you that I felt a little better. Dad then reminisced about a thirty-foot downhill putt I made to save par on 8 and then a great chip I hit on 11 from just off the green. I had totally forgotten about those good shots. It wasn't until then that I started to get what he was doing— and it was working! He chose to remember the good shots, and when my focus changed, so did my attitude.

Listen, we all make mistakes that we wish we hadn't. We're human; we make blunders out of pride, selfishness, and bad habits. In this golf example, I had allowed something so insignificant to give me stinkin' thinkin'. God knows we are a work in progress, and He has a fantastic plan for each of us. But His plan does not include you holding on to old cares and burdens. No! What He reminds us in times like these is the complete opposite. Listen to what it says in the gospel of John: "Peace I leave with you; my peace I give you. I do not give to you as the world gives. Do not let your hearts be troubled and do not be afraid" (14:27). This is such a great promise! You need to let these words sink deeply into your heart and soul. But if you allow bad memories to stay at the forefront of your mind, the torment you experience will take its toll on you and those around you. Thank goodness there's a better way—God's way! Just follow these three steps:

1. *Go to your* 2 Chairs *and talk it over with God.* Leave nothing out. That includes the real fears you're facing as well as all those wild imaginations about the worst things that *might* (but most likely will not) happen. God wants to hear all of it because He knows that your fears have the ability to take you hostage if you let them. Don't! Surrender them to God.

2. *Make the exchange!* That is, give Him the sadness, guilt, shame, disappointment, worry, or whatever is on your mind today. And then leave it with Him. Now, this is important: Don't walk in and pray about your problems each day and never make the exchange. If you do, you will miss out on the peace, joy, insight, wisdom, power, and favor that God promises He will give you. You *can* trust Him. His perfect peace will calm every circumstance and give you courage and strength to wait for His perfect timing.

3. *Thank Him in advance for helping you!* Even if there are still tough times ahead, being thankful in the midst of your trouble has an amazing effect on your attitude, on everyone around you, as well as on your confidence to claim victory over the trouble. Trust Him and then: order yourself . . . eyes forward!

When facing troubling times, these three tips are game changers. When you bring all your cares to God at *2 Chairs*, He will prepare you to take the bull by the horns and bring down your past hurts and future fears. You will be victorious once you're able to stop focusing on what's wrong and start remembering the good and what's going right. Otherwise, you'll remain paralyzed from the neck up. When people ask me for career advice, I tell them the first step is to maintain a "now focus" in their lives. The past is gone, and we can't relive it. All we have is today. As my dad always said: "Focus on the *now* not the *later*."

When I graduated from Southern Methodist University, I joined Carnation Company, which is now owned by Nestlé. I started in sales for their food service business in Dallas. One of the product lines we carried was frozen french fries. We sold them to distributors, who in turn sold them to restaurant chains like Dairy Queen and Hardees, as well as school districts and hospitals. I'll never forget my first big sale; it was on what we called a "Mad Monday." I should have known that such a name would be a foreshadowing of trouble.

> When you bring all your cares to God at *2 Chairs*, He will prepare you to take the bull by the horns and bring down your past hurts and future fears.

Fries are sold by the case on pallets and are shipped by trucks or railcars. Well, believe it or not, I sold an entire railcar of french fries to one customer. Not just one hundred cases, which I would have been happy about, but an entire railcar! I was pumped. When I told my boss, Tim (who for some reason never liked me much), even he was surprised and pleased. A railcar would have me in the running for salesperson of the month.

But then—*surprise!*—I got a call that Friday from my distributor whom I had sold the fries to. His first comment wasn't, "Hi, Bob. How are you?" It was, "What in the heck did you do?"

I said, "What do you mean?"

He shared that when he received the bill for the railcar, it seems I had not told him about any freight cost that needed to be added to the price of the fries. Being new in sales, I missed that "small" detail. To say it lightly, he was furious. He said he had already called my boss's boss to say that he expected us to honor the original price I'd quoted. And then hung up.

That's when my immediate boss, Tim, called to tell me I was an idiot and that I would probably have to pay the difference out my salary, if I was lucky enough to keep my job. He went on to say that our regional manager, Don, wanted to see me Monday morning at eight sharp to discuss this screw-up. At that moment, I realized that my celebration train had been derailed.

Trouble comes suddenly, doesn't it? Sometimes we bring it on, and other times it just hits us out of left field. But when it does, all the panic, defense mechanisms, frustration, and anger that come rushing in do us no good. I didn't know what to do. I called my dad to ask for advice, but he was in a meeting. So I called my mom, who I knew would lovingly encourage me and say everything was okay. Her response caught me off guard, though. After I explained my dire situation, she wasn't fazed by it at all. In fact, her response was the opposite of how a person would naturally respond. She exclaimed that this was a fantastic opportunity for me to trust God. *Huh?* Her advice was for me to go to my *2 Chairs* as fast as possible, tell God my situation, and then listen for His plan. Her advice was so direct and simple, and she believed with childlike faith that I would get the answer I needed.

What have you done with your trouble? Many hang on to it, try to handle it themselves, get isolated, and then become depressed. Most have never even heard of *2 Chairs*, and if someone were to suggest it to them, they might initially think it's pie-in-the-sky thinking. And I have to admit, I wasn't too keen on it following my fries fiasco. But my mom rejected all that and reminded me that this was a much bigger choice today. She was tough with me and reminded me of the importance of talking with

God personally at *2 Chairs*—every day, regardless of my circumstances. It wasn't about religion—it was about relationship. It was about knowing Him so well that I could confidently go directly to the Source of all answers and hear from Him myself. "When I do this," she said, "it changes the trajectory of my life. Anything less," she warned me, "would be me trying to be God for all my problems."

So here was the choice: Look in the rearview mirror, be the victim, and let my first big career challenge defeat me. Or consider doing something outlandish: order myself . . . eyes forward, believing that God is able to handle any problem I give Him at *2 Chairs*.

I fought many battles in my mind that weekend. It was as if there was an opponent whispering in my ear all the possible negatives to this situation like:

- "You should have known better."
- "You're a disappointment."
- "You'll probably get fired for this!"

But to my amazement, I was able to resist the fears that were attempting to clog up my thinking and instead cried out loud that I trusted God. I knew that He is bigger than I and way bigger than *any* problem, including this crisis at work. When I gave it all to Him, my fears diminished. This is such a great lesson to remember. From time to time, we all hear these voices but don't know what to do with them. Unfortunately, some people in crisis have become so accustomed to these voices that they don't even notice the intrusion. They let negative self-talk sneak in and ruin their day, week, month, or year. What I've learned and want to share with you is that you don't have to put up with this. At your *2 Chairs* and by reading God's Word, you'll find, as I did, that God has given you the authority to reject all that negative self-talk.

When I arrived at the office Monday morning, it felt as if a month had gone by since Friday. I had hoped all my problems would be solved before I got there, but when Tim met me at the door, he said that I should have known better. *Ugh! Thanks for the word of encouragement.* As I sat waiting to meet the big boss, I felt as though I was back in the principal's office about to be given detention . . . and the battle was raging in my mind again. However, I chose once again to believe this was God's battle, not mine, and somehow He was going to work a miracle for me in the next few minutes. And I have to tell you that this is such a powerful word for you to hear right now if you're in deep trouble. Don't succumb to the fear; face it! Ask God to give you the strength and courage we talked about in the last chapter, and then stand up to your fears and declare that they will not take you down one more minute.

Tim called me into Don's office, but to my surprise,

Don wasn't as mad at me as I thought he would be. First, he wanted to hear all the facts of the situation. Tim chimed in to give me a slap but only to hear Don ask him, "Isn't Bob new in sales, Tim? Where was your guidance and mentoring here? This was a big order. I would have thought you would have double-checked Bob's paperwork to be sure it was all in order." Needless to say, we didn't hear a peep from Tim the rest of the meeting, or the day.

What happened next has made an indelible mark on my life. Don asked his assistant to come in, and when she did she handed him a fax that she had just received from Carnation headquarters in Los Angeles. He peered at it over his glasses. He then asked me if I had given my distributor the price cut promotion we had going on that month for frozen french fries. The promotion was two dollars off a case. I said I hadn't even heard about it and just sold the fries at regular price. He smiled and said that was "good selling." Then, he

Don't succumb to the fear; face it!

got his calculator out and said something that warmed my heart, "Bob, the savings we could pass on to your distributor for the promotion going on right now more than covers the freight cost." *BOOM!* Problem solved.

As I left the office, I went out into the corridor and found a secluded spot around the corner and took a knee.

I was actually so overwhelmed by my prayer being answered that I just felt I needed to kneel down and thank God for His amazing help. My next call was to my mom. If you could have only heard her voice. She was so excited to hear what God had just done. I learned something fantastic that weekend. It's that our times of trouble are really opportunities to learn to trust God. It's the same with our burdens, cares, and problems. David reminds us in Psalm 55:22 to "Cast your cares on the LORD and he will sustain you; he will never let the righteous fall." The literal use of word *cast* was to throw a blanket on the back of a donkey, in the same way we would throw a saddle on a horse today. Imagine how crazy it would be to carry a saddle as we walked alongside

> **Our times of trouble are really opportunities to learn to trust God. It's the same with our burdens, cares, and problems.**

our horse. No, the saddle goes on the horse, and we mount up. We need to do that with our cares. The longer we try to carry them ourselves, the more problematic they will become.

I understand that giving up your cares isn't always easy, but if you've gotten to the *2 Chairs* by faith, don't leave without taking the next step and giving Him *all* your cares. He won't let you slip, fall, or fail. No, God says that "He will sustain you." Now, I can't tell you that the answer always comes in the package or the specific timing you want, but I can tell you from experience that I have never been disappointed when I was patient and trusted Him with my burdens and cares. What do you have to lose? Carrying them yourself never works out well.

The first time I heard about *2 Chairs* from my mom, it was almost too big for me to grasp. But once I started showing up every morning desiring to actually listen to God rather than just hear myself talk, that's when I began hearing His voice. Psalm 32:8 is one of my favorite verses. It says, "I will instruct you and teach you in the way you should go; I will counsel you and watch over you." Wow! Can you imagine that God Himself is personally going to instruct, teach, and guide you through your struggles? Test this and see for yourself.

When trouble came my way at Carnation Company, I understood why my mom had been so eager for me to go to my *2 Chairs*. She was right—it was a great opportunity for me to strengthen my relationship with God as I committed this situation to Him, trusting that He was able to handle it without me worrying and stressing about it.

As you sit in *2 Chairs* with God and decide to cast your burdens on Him, listen to what He says. It will be something like this, "Come on, let's go! Follow Me. Order yourself . . . eyes forward!"

When you do, you'll be ready for the next step, to "Do the Done!"

9

STEP #7
"DO THE DONE"

Be of good cheer.

—*John 16:33 kjv*

One of my favorite lines from the Bible is John 16:33, which I highly encourage you to memorize. It gives a forewarning about life in general that God wants you to know. It says, "In this world you will have trouble. But take heart [have confidence, be courageous, be of good cheer]! I have overcome the world."

I know what you're thinking. *Why would I like that quote, let alone memorize it? No one likes a quote that talks about impending trouble.* Well, I get that, but it's not the impending trouble part that has me so excited. It's that

God says something so incredible here, and we all need to hear it.

Let's review the three things He says:

1. In this world you will have trouble.
2. Take heart (or have confidence, be courageous, be of good cheer)!
3. I have overcome the world.

Of the three things, there is one specific thing that He wants and requires you to do at all times. And I never hear anyone talk about it because it sounds crazy. In fact, it's the complete opposite of how we normally respond to trouble, which is typically to moan, worry, get mad, or play the role of the victim. Of course this only drains our energy, splashes mud on everyone around us, and if it happens at work could even get us fired. What is it we're supposed to do instead? *Be of good cheer!* Huh? Why would I do that? Because He told you something good about this crisis you are in, and because of that you can choose to be cheerful in the face of that trouble—and that is a big statement. It lets Him and everyone around you know that you believe and trust Him. But you might say, "Hold it a second. I'm hurting. If you only knew the trouble I was in!" Well, I've got some news for you.

- He does know your situation.
- It's not too hard for Him to handle.
- And He has a good plan for you!

This is where knowing Who you believe in during tough times becomes so very powerful. To be cheerful in times like these, you have to know *something* about this situation that others just don't know. You have to have some insider information. Information that will encourage you not to just be able to hang in there but to be so confident in the midst of the trouble that people around you are awestruck and are talking about this attitude of yours.

I'll never forget the first time I went to a haunted house. Just before I paid my two dollars to walk in, my older brother, Bill, pulled me aside and asked me if I had ever been in a haunted house before. I told him no. He said, "Now listen, when you go inside, there are going to be a lot of people made up in scary outfits and painted faces, flashing lights, and eerie music. And just when you don't expect it, then somebody is going to jump out at you and scream. Their main goal is to try to scare you. It's what they do! But listen—don't be scared; it's just for fun. Are you okay with this?" I nodded at him, but Bill said, "No, you got to tell me verbally that you heard this warning and are okay with this."

I said, "Okay!" I paid my two dollars, and as soon as I walked in, a person who was hidden behind the door jumped out and scared the you-know-what out of me! I can definitely see why people get frightened at haunted houses.

But because my brother had forewarned me, it changed my attitude, my approach; in fact, it changed the entire experience for me. What's interesting is that nothing in the haunted house that I walked through that day had changed. The people, darkness, music, flashing lights, and scary figures were all still there. But the insider information I had received beforehand had changed me so I could respond differently than I would have otherwise. Once I got past that first scare, I was able to remember the warning that this would be scary but not dangerous. I was able to rely on my brother's assurance that everything in there was all for fun. From that moment on I was more prepared. Yes, I still got startled occasionally, but I just laughed and moved throughout the house in a much more courageous and cheerful way.

In the same way, some people are really frightened of stormy weather. Now I'm not talking about hurricanes or tornados but more the normal thunderstorms and heavy rain that come our way each year. Back in Chicago, where I grew up, my dad taught our family to love thunderstorms. We'd sit out on our screened-in porch and watch for lightning and then count the seconds before the thunder cracked to see how far away it was. Dad and Mom always made us feel relaxed and safe in the middle of bad weather. I remember them jokingly saying that God was probably bowling a strike up in heaven when we'd hear the loud crack of thunder. I'm sure bad weather is probably very scary for many people, but for us it was awesome and actually a lot of fun to experience. Watching how much Mom and Dad enjoyed a storm has changed our perspective of storms ever since.

Is it possible so many common fears—like getting on an airplane, bad weather, heights, tight places, crowds, animals, being alone, and the list could go on forever—could have been altered if only we had received a forewarning like the one I got from my brother Bill at the haunted house? Wouldn't life be easier to navigate if people put a positive spin on negative events in the same way my mom and dad made thunderstorms such a good thing when we were growing up? I believe so!

Well, the Bible couldn't be more straightforward in forewarning everyone who lives on this planet that from time to time—and often without warning—trouble will come our way. It's just part of life. But God also gave us a response to all the trouble we face. What was it?

- "Be of good cheer!"
- "Be courageous!"
- "Take heart and be confident!"

But how can we react this way when the situation looks impossible? Well, that's what I mean by "Do the Done."

God has some good news: He has already won! It is finished! He has overcome the world and everything that you're facing. And if you accept this assignment and face the trouble in front of you with "good cheer," you're in for the ride of your life.

Growing up I loved watching the television show *Mission: Impossible*, and ever since then, I've loved the *Mission: Impossible* movies even more because of the trouble Tom Cruise's character faces and all his fantastical escapes. Each movie starts with a message that says something like this, "If you accept the assignment, you will have to follow the clues, the markings, and the plan even though it might look IMPOSSIBLE at times to follow." How impossible? Extremely! Within seconds of the movie starting, there's always a constant flow of trouble. In life, we often feel that same kind of tension: the realization that some friends are not really our friends at all; a bad health prognosis; time in jail for us or a loved one; a relationship that's gone wrong; or the death of a loved one. This all happens to us in a matter of seconds during our "movie" called life, and we don't know how long a scene will last or when the closing credits will roll. And, like most movies, before we reach the end, we can expect multiple moments of setback, frustration, disillusion, despair, and then even more major setbacks—all this to make the plot more intriguing. Does this sound familiar? Of course it does. It sounds like life as we know it.

Every epic story, comeback, or miracle we have loved watching or reading about throughout history has always had *one thing* in common: T-R-O-U-B-L-E. And lots of it! In fact, the bigger the problem and the more outrageous the trouble, the more enjoyable it is watching the movie. That's so true when it comes to movies . . . but not so much when it's unfolding in our lives. Or is it? Is it possible that our lives are one more epic story and all of the troubles, all the setbacks we've been experiencing or will experience are just opportunities to get to "epiphany moments" when we realize that our search for answers outside of God is fruitless? It's true that most times in life we have no control over the circumstances that come our way, but we do have a say in our attitudes—and we need to change them before we can allow our hero, God Himself, to show up on our behalf and help us through each crisis.

Another epic movie I love is *Rudy*. Of all the great scenes I could share, the one I like the most is where Rudy is sitting in the church contemplating his BIG problem. It's as if God Himself wrote this scene so that you and I would know exactly what to do when trouble knocks on our door. Read carefully here. I don't want you to miss this.

If you haven't seen the movie, it's about a guy, Rudy,

who wants to get into Notre Dame and walk on the football team. Okay, that doesn't sound too impossible until we quickly find out that Rudy lacks the grades, the money, and is "five-foot-nothin', one hundred and nothin', and [has] barely a speck of athletic ability." I love movies like this. Rudy doesn't want to just play football; no, he wants to play at Notre Dame, one of the best teams in the country. Add to it that there are multiple other problems hidden along the way and time is running out.

In this scene the priest who has been trying to help Rudy get into Notre Dame walks into the church and sees him sitting in a pew and asks him, "Making an appeal to the Higher Court?"

And Rudy says, "I'm desperate. If I don't get into Notre Dame next semester, it's over; it's done."

Have you ever said something like that? In the midst of your trouble, you start thinking the worst about your situation and then blurt out loud, "If I don't get an answer to my problem right now, it's over; it's done." My friend, please don't say that, because it's not over and it's not done! It's *never* over or done until God says it's over and done. And what He said is this: "Do the Done!" Let me show you.

The priest tries to console Rudy by telling him that, so far, he's done a great job chasing down his dream. Rudy responds, "What good is it if all my effort doesn't produce results? It doesn't mean anything." That's how we think in times of trouble, don't we? We go to church and we pray, but if we don't get the answers that we want immediately, we start to complain or pick up our toys and leave.

The priest reminds Rudy of something that's really, really hard for all of us to recognize in times of trouble: "Praying is something we do in our time; answers come in God's time." I'm sure Rudy didn't want to hear that. Who would?

Rudy asks him, "Have I done everything I possibly can? Can you help me?"

The priest has a great response to Rudy in his time of trouble. He says, "Son, in thirty-five years of religious study, I've come up with only two hard, incontrovertible facts: there is a God, and I'm not Him."

It's *never* over or done until God says it's over and done. And what He said is this: "Do the Done!"

Wow, isn't that interesting? Now, I have to tell you that for years I had watched that scene, and each time I was bothered at the end, thinking the priest kind of left Rudy hanging without a solution to his trouble. But, over the years, I've realized that I missed what he was saying all along.

Rudy was in the right place, at the right time . . . but asking the *wrong person* for help. He should have gone to *2 Chairs* and spoken to God directly. Isn't that so common today? In times of trouble, we panic and start talking to everyone *but* God. We call all the "experts" we know—those who have specific knowledge, skills, or financial resources that could help us. Rudy went to the priest, the most prominent person he knew in the local Catholic church. "Networking" with him to get a recommendation seemed like the logical thing to do at the time. But what if the problems are bigger or more complex, such as an incurable disease, a love that's gone out of a marriage, or a child in trouble with drugs or alcohol? Or what if the problem is one that you just don't have any control over whatsoever? What do you do then? *2 Chairs*!

I wrote in the Introduction about how my mom shared with me the secret of *2 Chairs*, but did you wonder how she discovered that for herself? A little family history might be helpful.

My mom grew up as a Methodist in Norfolk, Virginia. She made a decision to follow the Lord early in her life, I'm sure not knowing what an impact it would make on so many people later in her life. She met my dad just before World War II started. He was a strapping young second lieutenant in the navy and she was working for the naval department's war office. Dad was from New York and a graduate of Notre Dame, and Mom was a Southern belle going to William & Mary. They met, fell in love, and married in a short period of time.

After a two-week honeymoon in New York, Dad was shipped off to war for a year and a half. Can you believe it? All of a sudden, he was on a destroyer in the South Pacific. It was a dangerous ship to be on during that time, as far too many similar ships went out but never came back. They wrote each other three times a day, every day, and numbered each letter. In these letters, they actually got to know each other, shared their love, their dreams, and prayed to God that they could be together once again, start a family, and build a wonderful life.

After the war ended, my mom and dad did just that— they started a family in South Bend, Indiana. They had four children, Frank Jr., Bill, Nancy, and me. My dad was a McKinsey consultant back then, so he had to travel Monday through Friday trying to start a career while Mom stayed home with us kids. Dad saw quickly that this type of travel was too hard on the family and caused too much stress and trouble at home. With Dad on the road so much, there was less opportunity for him to help us kids with our homework, not to mention no consistent fatherly mentoring. It soon became obvious that trying to build character in kids by telephone and just on weekends wasn't working. It wasn't long before Dad decided to change jobs and move out of South Bend.

We first moved to Los Angeles and then to Chicago. As they are today, moves were tough on our family. We lived in Southern California for six years before my dad decided to pack us all up and head to Chicago to start a new industry called "executive search." It was a good move but, again, it took its toll. Add to that the seventies came and with it a changing culture of drugs and rock 'n' roll. Suddenly, families just like ours all across the country were faced with a dilemma: how to adjust to all these new "freedoms" and changes.

Now I share our family story to give you and the current generation a small glimpse of that time. It was a great generation that won World War II and then was busy building, traveling, and working. But something happened with all that busyness. The spiritual leadership role in families seemed to shift from dads to moms, along with everything else they were doing. Between the three-martini business lunches that dads were having during work and all the problems moms were handling at home (without much help from their husbands), it's understandable how families encountered strife and issues that weren't so simple to handle, no less solve.

As a member of the Greatest Generation, my dad held his relationship with God in the same importance as being an American citizen. For him, loving God meant praying, walking with integrity, following the Ten Commandments, and trying to do his best. But because Dad only scheduled God for Sundays and daily prayers, something was clearly missing. At the same time, my mom was taking the lead raising four kids, trying to hang in there with the stress of moves, and doing everything she could to encourage my dad as he started a new business—all the while hearing these quiet messages from God: "Martha, there is something more! Are you interested?"

So one morning at four, my mom woke up burdened, as she described it, with such a heaviness of heart. It drove her out of bed and downstairs to the sunroom, her favorite place to retreat and enjoy some quiet. Have you ever felt that? I'm sure you have. Trouble has a way of tugging at your heart so hard that you almost can't breathe. You just have to get up and do something about it.

> **My dad held his relationship with God in the same importance as being an American citizen. But something was clearly missing.**

My mom knew that feeling well because she first experienced it when she was eleven, after her dad died unexpectedly. It was a devastating blow to her and the whole family. Suddenly she was without an anchor and felt all alone, but she cried out to God. She heard Him say to her, "Martha, I'm right here. Let's talk." So, at a young age, she discovered *2 Chairs*. Then, in the midst of one of the lowest moments of her life, she felt a covering, a peace that passed all understanding, and an empowerment to face her fears. After that, talking with God in this way became a habit, and the best time for that to occur was early in the morning before the sun rose. It was then they would talk about the plans for the day.

But now, years later, Mom was thinking, *How did I let it go?* She missed her time with Him, those *2 Chairs* moments together. Somehow she had gotten so busy with the cares of the world and all that was going on having to raise four kids that she stopped meeting with Him before the day got started. She would still go to church, but she had accepted the familiarity of religion over relationship. Have you done that? It's not hard to do.

So in the sunroom that morning, she wept as she experienced the same feelings she had felt when she was younger. With tears flowing, thinking about all the cares of the world that had been crashing down on her and the family, she started talking out loud to God. "What should I do?" She was just speaking out to God somewhere, out there, when she heard God's voice coming from the chair to her left.

"Martha. I'm over here. Let's talk."

My mom didn't see a glow from heaven, there was no music from angels, nor did she see Him physically in the other chair. But she knew His voice. You will too. I don't know if she heard Him audibly or just in her mind, but it didn't matter. It was the most exciting, exhilarating thing she said that had ever happened to her. And she didn't want it to end. In that quiet time, God and my mom spoke. And you can too! No one can get in the way of that. He told her that He knew her situation and not to worry. My mom told me that love seemed to have engulfed the room. She said the problems that had looked so big a few minutes earlier had all of a sudden seemed so small, so insignificant.

God told my mom, "It's time for a change, Martha. You need to give Me all your cares and worries, all your hopes and dreams, the whole load. When you do, your family will see the difference in you. And even though the problems may still seem the same, the joy and confidence you will receive from Me here will give

My mom didn't see a glow from heaven, there was no music from angels, nor did she see Him physically in the other chair. But she knew His voice. You will too.

you strength to overcome." He then asked my mom, "Do you believe?"

My mom said, "Yes, I believe; help my unbelief!"

In the spring of 1976, after I finished my junior year at SMU, I went home to Chicago. When I walked through the front door, I could feel immediately that something was different. It just felt brighter, more positive. I didn't know exactly what it was, but there was very definitely something good going on. And then I saw my mom, and I knew that God had to be involved. How did I know? You just had to look at her. Her countenance, outlook, and perspective were so joyful, peaceful, and happy. When I told her that she looked five years younger, she just beamed.

When I told my dad how happy and how much younger Mom looked, he agreed but didn't know why. He thought my mom was going through her time of life. It's so funny looking back at this now, because what was so impactful to my dad was that she didn't try to change him; she just loved him through his difficult times. She had the faith to "Do the Done," to let go and believe that if she did her part, trusting and believing, God would do *His* part with my dad and the family.

The simple faith that my mom exercised was so attractive to my dad that it wasn't too long before he was doing *2 Chairs* himself. And when he did, the change in him was even more unbelievable than it was with my mom. Now, with the two of them united, their example to the family was beyond impactful. One by one, each of us in the family wanted that peace they had, and one by one, in God's perfect timing, we each received it.

I want to encourage and inspire you about your challenges ahead and the all-important choices you must make to solve them. Remember these three simple words: "Do the Done." The choice is who you will follow: God's system or the world's? It is important to know how the two approaches are so diametrically opposite.

Tom Ziglar, the son of legendary Zig Ziglar, is a great *WHO* friend I do regular breakfasts with to discuss ideas like this. Tom is one of the most caring, thoughtful, and wisest people I know. Sometimes when we're inspiring each other with stories, our breakfast times can leave planet Earth and rise to heights that I just can't explain.

When I first brought the *2 Chairs* idea to Tom, he was ecstatic. I talked about the *exchange* we can make each morning with God, letting go of our troubles and daily concerns and, in turn, receiving God's peace, joy, insight, wisdom, power, and favor for the day. Tom said his dad would have loved this book. Zig always said, "You plus God equals enough." But Tom added something interesting that God had also been sharing with me at *2 Chairs*: "Spending this time with God activates four things in our life: *hope, optimism, creativity,* and then *the plan.* Each step is progressive." Let's review both systems.

God's System

- **Hope:** God has "overcome the world" and won the victory!

- **Optimism:** God knows our situation, and it's not too hard for Him to handle!
- **Creativity:** God takes us to higher ground and unlocks great and mighty things inside us.
- **The Plan:** God has a great plan for us and wants to share it!

I told Tom that morning that the world's system also has an exchange for trouble and daily concerns as well as four steps it recommends for a better life. The only problem is, this plan only brings temporary relief rather than a lasting one. The exchange the world's approach makes for trouble and daily concerns is masked by drugs, excessive alcohol, horoscopes, and mindless entertainment. The biggest difference in the world's four steps is that the order is inverted from that of God's steps. It doesn't start out with *hope* but with *the plan*. Each step is also progressive.

The World's System

- **The Plan:** It's not personal and was not designed with you in mind. People you don't know and who are supposedly smarter than you came up with it.
- **Creativity:** A select few design, create, and showcase what's in and what's not. You weren't invited, but if you are, only inside-the-box ideas are recognized.

- **Optimism:** "Houston, we have a problem!" With divorce, debt, crime, terrorism, sickness, and unemployment rampant, optimism has left the station.
- **Hope:** People are looking in all the wrong places.

As I close, let me give you a practical example of this. When I started writing this book, I didn't start with a plan. I started with God at *2 Chairs*. One morning during our talk time, I heard Him say, "It's time to write about what we are doing each day."

I immediately felt the pressure of having to write a book like this. I told Him, "I'm not a priest or pastor. I'm an executive recruiter."

He immediately said, "Don't worry about that; give that to Me." He then asked me, "Do you trust Me?"

"Yes, but . . . when will I find the time? This is such a big subject—what if I let you down?"

I could almost hear Him laugh. "Bob, we've done this before. All I need you to do is what I've already done. Are you with Me? Will you 'Do the Done'?"

"Yes," I responded. "I am with You!" It was then, right there at our *2 Chairs,* when *hope* flooded me and then *optimism, creativity*, and *the plan* followed. A plan He would reveal only day by day at our *2 Chairs*!

This is just the beginning
of what I believe
you will soon experience
with God at *2 Chairs*.
Please don't delay!
He has so much
He wants to tell you.

10

SEE YOU TOMORROW

I will come down and speak with you there.

—Numbers 11:17

Well, we've covered a lot of ground. Let's take a breath and think about the magnitude of the opportunity at hand—to sit and "tabernacle" with God each morning. I love that word *tabernacle* because it's a word from ancient days that means a "place of meeting" or a "tent" where God dwelt among His people. For some reason, many have no problem believing that God met with people personally back then, but they're not so sure He does it today. I hope this book has been, and will continue to be, a reminder that He is the same yesterday, today, and forever. He's never changed, and He never will. Remember the secret: God, the Creator of all things, desires a deep and intimate relationship with *you*. And right now, as you are reading this sentence, He is calling you to *2 Chairs*.

For some of you, this concept is fresh, exciting, and could not have come at a better time. For some who have been doing morning devotions for years, *2 Chairs* is a new way to think about your daily time with God. And, for others, I know all of this might seem outrageous. What I love about the three simple but disruptive questions is that they bring us all to the same conclusion.

- Does God know your situation? Yes!
- Is it too hard for Him to handle? No!
- Does He have a good plan for you? Yes!

What is the plan? Oops, we don't know. Exactly! You need to allow God to reveal His plan for you—daily!—at *2 Chairs*. Isn't it obvious that to get to know God, to learn to trust Him, and to let Him lead us, we must regularly spend time with Him? The more time we spend telling Him our fears and dreams and the more time we spend listening to Him in the quiet of our mornings, the better we will get to know Him.

We already do that with our best friends, don't we? We have a close relationship with them, which is quite different from our relationship with others we know. It's as if we speak back and forth on a special frequency that we only share with those closest to our hearts: our *WHO* friends. We are dialed in to what seems to always matter most to one another. When we're together, our lives are enriched and seem to be on "enhanced mode."

Well, whatever it is that you might have experienced with your friends or family, I can tell you from experience that a conversation with God is exponentially better. And this starts by you giving your first moments to Him each day. Why? Because He has some specific instructions, strategies, and encouragement that He'd like to share with you. Sometimes you'll hear Him say, "I'm sending someone across your path whom I need you to encourage. Don't miss this." It could be a small change in an attitude or preparation He wants you to make for an upcoming project. You won't likely be able to use last week's strategies or words today. But don't worry; God has tender mercies, which are new every morning, and He wants to give you fresh peace, joy, insight, wisdom, power, and favor each new day.

The reason I encourage you to go to *2 Chairs* before you start each day is because you need to put God's thoughts and words into your mind and heart first so you can spend the rest of the day walking in His light and sharing His love. I'm telling you, your day will change BIG TIME if you start with *2 Chairs* and then spend the rest of the day working His plan that He gives you.

In days of old, God showcased this daily provision for His people out in the desert. He provided them a sweet food, fresh each morning, called "manna." He did this so they could travel through uninhabitable places and not have to be concerned with growing, buying, or carrying their food. He promised that they'd never be hungry. But the food was only good for one day. They couldn't save it for the next or it would rot. God was teaching them to cling to Him each and every day for *new manna*, which He joyfully provided—and He also wants to provide for you daily at *2 Chairs*.

> Your day will change BIG TIME if you start with *2 Chairs* and then spend the rest of the day working His plan.

As I mentioned earlier, my mom was eleven when she started to hear these daily messages from God. Unfortunately, when life got more complicated and busy in her adult life, she stopped spending those first few minutes with God each morning. It wasn't until she was in her forties that she decided it was time once again to sit down with God each morning. Sure enough, He was waiting and eager to hear my mom share her heart's desires, hopes, and fears so He could once again give her peace and inspiration through His comforting words.

But there's more. God used these times with my mom to bring peace and joy to our home in a way that was real.

When you were young, did you ever notice that you liked going to one relative's house more than another's? Maybe it was the smell, the food, or the attitudes of your cousins. Whatever caused it be your favorite, in reality, wasn't it the *feel* you got walking in the house?

When she was a little girl, my oldest daughter, Aly, used to tell me how much she loved staying over at my mom and dad's house. She told me that there was a peace, a feeling of love as if she were being hugged the moment she walked in the front door. I now understand that feeling was all created with *2 Chairs*. My mom's habit of starting each day, welcoming the presence of God into her house, established an enduring peaceful atmosphere everyone, even her young granddaughter, clearly felt.

Now that Aly is married and has two boys of her own, she has tried to make the *2 Chairs* habit her daily time with God. And the result impacts everyone who enters her house, just as it did when she went over to her grandma and grandpa's house so many years ago.

The day following my mom's eightieth birthday party, she called me to say her back was hurting. She said she had slipped on some water when she got home following the celebration but didn't want to bother me, even though I lived only a few blocks away. That morning, though, she asked if I could come over.

My mom was a young eighty, active with friends, still

driving, and doing her own thing without concern. When I arrived, I could see immediately that her back was tight. I took her over to the doctor, and he said it was a slight bruise. But over the next five days it seemed to get worse. She couldn't get in and out of bed easily, and it was very difficult for her to get around. After taking her back to the doctor, he gave her some anti-inflammatory pills and told her to put a heating pad on it from time to time.

The next day when I arrived, I could see Mom's attitude had changed. She was still in a lot of pain, but she was much more determined. I thought that was good. I asked her how she had slept and she said she had long conversations with God at her *2 Chairs*. That's when my mom said that she had come to a decision: "If this keeps hurting, I am going to tell God to take me home."

I said, "What? No! You can tell God you'll be ready at ninety-seven, maybe, but not eighty!"

"Listen, everything is okay with all the kids, and I miss your dad and would love to meet God and see heaven."

"No way! Mom, your back is just bruised."

All she said next was, "I'm just telling you."

I immediately called my sister Nancy, who also lived close by, to tell her what Mom had said: "If she doesn't feel better, she's going to tell God to bring her home." Now this whole conversation would not have fazed me, but because my mom had such a great relationship with God at her

2 Chairs, I knew that He might just "do it" for her—if she asked. I told my sister to come over pronto. She talked it all through with Mom, and all seemed better. I told my mom as I left that I'd come over and check on her the next morning after I finished a breakfast meeting.

I rang the doorbell the next morning. No answer. I knocked. Nothing. I thought maybe she couldn't hear me because she was in the backyard, so I let myself in using the key I had. As I walked in, it only took three steps before I felt God stop me. I heard Him say, "Bob, your mom is sitting with Me right now. Don't be afraid. Before you go around the corner, guard your heart." I was stunned! I ran in and saw her. She was sitting in her chair and her eyes and mouth were wide open with an expression like she had just seen a long-lost friend. Her two arms were reaching out as if she was greeting that friend with a hug. Did she just tell me yesterday she was going home? Did she just call her shot in the corner pocket? She did!

Sitting there next to her at that moment was surprisingly not scary. Why? Because all my life Mom had talked to me about how amazing going to heaven would be. She couldn't wait to meet God, see

> It only took three steps before I felt God stop me. I heard Him say, "Bob, your mom is sitting with Me right now."

Dad, her parents, and all those who went before her who knew the "secret"—that we can know Him *before* we get there. I'm sure as she entered heaven she heard God say, "Martha, I'm right over here!"

What kind of reasons or thoughts have kept you from getting to know God at *2 Chairs*?

- Do you think you're too busy? *Make the time!*
- Do you think it's too late to begin? *You're never too late!*
- Does your situation feel hopeless? *God is the source of your hope, and through Him all things are possible!*
- Do you feel that you're too messed up to talk to God? *God loves you and wants you just as you are—not a future version of you!*
- Have you "tried prayer" before and don't believe it will work? *You'll find this time different!*

I don't know how to describe the indescribable. In fact, I couldn't even give you a preview of the epic story God wants to write in and through your life because I wouldn't want the limitations of my words to understate the enormity He has ahead for you.

I have written everything that God has put on my heart to share with you, but it's not the end. This is just the beginning of what I believe you will soon experience with God at *2 Chairs*. Please don't delay! He has so much He wants to tell you. With all that's going on in the world as well as at home, meeting God at *2 Chairs* will be transformational for you. But remember, epic stories have lots of ups and downs, twists and turns. When you face them, ask yourself those *three simple but disruptive questions* and then get started putting into practice each of the seven practical steps. Don't be discouraged if a problem you face isn't solved immediately—just trust in God's daily invitation to *2 Chairs*. Remember what my mom told you God would say: "See you tomorrow! Same place, same time."

> I don't know how to describe the indescribable. . . . I wouldn't want the limitations of my words to understate the enormity He has ahead for you.

ACKNOWLEDGMENTS

The acknowledgments section of a book is my favorite. It's an opportunity to thank each of my *WHO* friends for helping me get this book in your hands.

First thanks, of course, goes to God! For always sitting next to me every day, loving, mentoring, guiding, and helping me each step of the way. You are so good! You've never let me down. Knowing *You* is my goal and prize.

Next, to the love of my life, Cheryl, who sometimes gets up earlier than I do just to get to *2 Chairs* first! Thank you. I love you! Writing a book takes time, and you made this experience special by listening to me night after night share every line, encouraging me, reminding me of old stories, and making brilliant suggestion. To my three incredible daughters, Aly, Jenny, and Rachel—I love you! You all inspire me each and every day. I'm so excited to share a story about each of you in this book. Can't wait until the day my three grandchildren—Maverick, Emma, and Major—can read this and start their *2 Chairs* adventure!

To my great friend George Brandon, thank you for encouraging me to write this book the first day you heard me talk about it and then inspiring me every day until it was finished! To Ruth Brandon, thanks for your encouragement and listening to George and me brainstorm all those hours.

To my close confidant and right hand at Eastman & Beaudine, Kevin Goll, you have to be singled-out, high-fived, and acknowledged for listening, elevating perspective, and providing your tremendous literary skills. Thank you for helping me make this simple message shine, and to Hillary for being *all in* on this project.

To my awesome sister, Nancy, who continues to be a clarifying sounding board in my life and was in this book as well. To my older brothers, Frank and Bill, thanks for a lifetime of memories that inspired this book. To both my sons-in-law: Donovan, thank you for your creative contributions, which made a huge difference; Rob, thank you for always allowing me to talk through new ideas with you.

To my close friend Tom Ziglar, special thanks for all our breakfasts where you inspired me (as your Dad did before you) to even greater heights at *2 Chairs*! You are such a giver and great *WHO*! Love ya, Tommy Z, and the whole Ziglar family and Legacy training team!

To my long-time book publishing friend Bruce Barbour for serving as my agent on this book as well as helping edit it. Thanks you for your confidence, encouragement, and passionate belief in *2 Chairs*. You and Karen Ann have been irreplaceable in making this book extraordinary.

To Byron Williamson and the superb creative team at Worthy Publishing—THANK YOU! Byron, you immediately saw the vision I had to get people all over the world to do their *2 Chairs* with God. You're a Moment Maker!

To so many great friends who patiently listened to me talk about *2 Chairs* over breakfasts, lunches, dinners, and phone calls over the years—thank you! Your input and encouragement was more valuable than you will ever know.

Finally, thank you to those who uniquely touched this book in their own special way including: my wonderful mother-in-law, Marjorie Whitaker, Andy Bowles, Mike and Karri Vaught, Bryan Sperber, Taylor Sexton, Kyle Eager, Taylor Brandon, Billy Cox, Jim Hoffman, Bob Akin, Dan Arnold and family, Kathleen Hessert, Jay Allison, Fran Fraschilla, Bob Hoffman, Jon Heidtke, George Killebrew, Robert Mawire (Do the Done!), Ray Davis, Ryan and Ellie Binkley and everyone at Create Church, Randy Frazee, Orlando and JoAnn Reyes, Larry North, Tom Klein, Mike Dickie, Rick Barfield, Greg Brown, Andy Rawlings, Rick George, Ricky Lefft, Danny McDaniel, Susan Mead, Bob Tiede, Taylor Smiley, Greg Economou, Chris Noonan, Chris Kleinert, Scott Wysong, Jared Mosley, Joe and Jen Parker, Jordan Bazant, Andrew

Berg, Amanda Skelte, Robin Blakeley, Will Brewer, June Jones, John Cahill, Jeremy Walls, Paul Teske, Michael Koulianos, Jim Donofrio, Cary and Laurie Turner, Keith Hackett, Mike Golub, Jack Graham, Jarrett Stephens, Jim Beckett, Joe Galindo, Ann Louden, and Doug McNamee.

ABOUT THE AUTHOR

Bob Beaudine is the president and CEO of Eastman & Beaudine and recognized as the top sports/entertainment search executive in the U.S. Beaudine also served as a member of the board of directors of the two-time American League Champion Texas Rangers. Bob and his wife, Cheryl, have been married over thirty years and have three grown daughters. They live in Plano, Texas.

Bob Beaudine is a sought-after keynote speaker
at corporations, non-profits, universities, conventions,
conferences, workshops, and churches.

Bob's corporate speaking clients have included:
Exxon-Mobil, Nike, Cessna, and AIG. Sports-industry
speeches have included: Learfield Sports, Madison
Square Garden, Los Angeles Lakers, and the Sports
Business Journal Motorsports Marketing Forum.
University speeches have included: University of
Oklahoma, Baylor University, University of California
at Berkley, and University of Memphis. Other speak-
ing highlights of Bob's have included: Oak Hills
Church in San Antonio, the NCAA Pathway Program,
the American Football Coaches Association, and the
Texas Conference for Women at the invitation of then-
First Lady Anita Perry.

If you would like to inquire about
Bob Beaudine speaking to your event or group,
please visit bobbeaudine.com.

Bob Beaudine is also the author of
The Power of WHO! and
The Power of WHO! Workbook.

In these books, Bob shows how achieving that place in life you always dreamed of isn't about who you don't know but who you're overlooking—the close friends you've been given who are pre-wired to help you in ways you never imagined.

The Power of WHO! is available at major book stores, online retailers, and as an audio book.
(Hachette Book Group, 2009)

The Power of WHO! Workbook is available exclusively in hard copy at bobbeaudine.com or as an eBook on Amazon.

IF YOU ENJOYED *2 CHAIRS*, WILL YOU CONSIDER SHARING THE MESSAGE WITH OTHERS?

Mention *2 Chairs* in a blog post or through Facebook, Twitter, or upload a picture through Instagram.

Recommend *2 Chairs* to those in your small group, book club, workplace, and classes.

Head over to facebook.com/BobBeaudine.WHO, "LIKE" the page, and post a comment as to what you enjoyed the most.

Tweet "I recommend reading #2ChairsSecret by @YouGotWho // @worthypub"

Pick up a copy for someone you know who would be challenged and encouraged by the *2 Chairs* message.

Write a book review online.

WORTHY® PUBLISHING

Visit us at worthypublishing.com

twitter.com/worthypub

youtube.com/worthypublishing

facebook.com/worthypublishing

instagram.com/worthypub